THE
FL*I*P SIDE
of Glory

Brandi Winans

Brandi. You are my sister in all of this. Like you said, you have to be an NFL wife to really understand what it is we (Sharon, Suzy, Autumn, Cindy, Elleanore, Karen and many, many more) have to face and stand up to on a daily basis. Congratulations on the success of your book, The Flip Side of Glory.

Gina Boyd

I met Brandi during the first "Independent Retired Player Summit" in Las Vegas, NV in 2009. As a former NFL player (1998-2002), I was impressed with her conviction and her ability to convey the reality of brain injuries as it relates to her husband and former NFL player. Her story not only opened my eyes to the potential reality of the game, but I believe that all fans and players of the game, at every level, can benefit from her experience.

Charles Kirby, Technical Recruiter (e-comm), Bond Street Group, LLCwas with another company when working with Brandi at D.F.O.C., Inc.

Brandi Winans has an amazing, inspirational true story that will motivate you to find a ray of hope for your life. I first met Brandi 33 years ago and the grand circle of life has now reunited us in a common cause to make the "right" difference in the human element. Her story will affect a very positive change in the life of anyone who is – stuck– and needs to move forward. Great work Brandi!! I'm honored to have you as a dear friend.

Kevin James Richardson, Life Coach, Motivational Speaker, Author, Promotional Consultant/Publisher, University of Washington was a consultant or contractor to Brandi at Day For Our Children, Inc.(D.F.O.C.)

THE
FL*I*P SIDE
of Glory

A true story of

Love, Acceptance and Hope

as told by an NFL Wife

Brandi Winans

Sirena Press

Other publications include:

The Wannabe Seminars

The Stepping Stones of Life

For information:
727-433-4842
www.brandiwinans.com
Livespeaker@aol.com

Cover and Book Design
theMurmaid ᵗᵐ
for Sirena Press

Printed in the United States of America
Second American Edition

Murmaid Publishing
Murmaid@tampabay.rr.com

Introduction

God surely works in mysterious ways. I met Brandi Winans in 2004 when I bought her home. Twenty-four hours after she first showed me her home, we attended The Passion of the Christ, then went upstairs for dinner and negotiated the terms of sale. We've been fast friends ever since.

It's my joy and pleasure to introduce this account of Brandi's life. In these pages you'll see her courage and her kindness as she tries to help her Super Bowl winning husband deal with his physical, emotional and prescription drug addiction while raising a wonderful son.

Brandi knows firsthand the consequences of multiple concussions on the personality and health of a football player. This is why she works tirelessly as an NFL Advocate for Retired Players Disability Pensions. She recently shared her experiences by giving written testimony before the U.S. Congress.

I know you'll find her passion–for life, for love, and for Christ–in these pages.

Joan Johnston
New York Times bestselling author of *A Stranger's Game*

Acknowledgements

First and foremost, I would like to give thanks to my Lord and Savior, Jesus Christ, for allowing me the privilege to write this book and glorify Him, my writing mentor, Nancy Frederich and my spiritual mentor, Cay Woodard, along with all my family and friends who have given me the inspirational tools to come full circle in my life.

Third, to Chris Nowinski, author of Head Games and Jeff, my former husband, who both helped me understand the on-going effects of major concussions and to Bryant Gumbel and HBO Real Sports for bringing an awareness of the devastating effects of concussions, and what the NFL spouses and families go through after our husbands leave the game.

Finally, to my friend and bestselling author, Joan Johnston, who gave me the strength to never give up on my dream of being able to tell this story of love, acceptance and hope.

Dedication

This book is dedicated to my former husband, Jeff, and our son, Travis (our greatest blessing) and to all the former NFL disabled and retired players and their families who suffer from physical and emotional disabilities, and who continue the fight for pensions, as well as payments for physical and emotional medical treatments. Forever we are one.

This book is also dedicated to the many caretakers, spouses and families of injured and disabled men, women and children. You are the real heroes. NEVER GIVE UP! With God on your side anything is possible. If God takes you to it, God will get you through it.

Preface

Like every little girl, I dreamed of meeting the man of my dreams, my "Prince Charming" and living happily ever after. My Prince Charming was Jeffrey Dow Winans, a Professional football player I met in the summer of 1979 while he was playing for the Tampa Bay Buccaneers. Successful, handsome and extremely confident, he seemed to have it all.

By July 1981, my Cinderella life came to an abrupt end, when Jeff became physically and then emotionally disabled from pro football. He was 30 years old. I was thrown into the role of rescuer, caretaker and sole-support of our family, while fighting the NFL to get Jeff's disability benefits. After fighting for his NFL disability benefits and being turned down for three years, in July, 1984, we finally won our case through NFL arbitration.

A few months after Jeff's temporary disability pension started, our lives were turned upside down again. After Jeff suffered a horrific gunshot accident, the NFL decided that he was no longer disabled from football, but from the gunshot accident and they took his disability pension away.

We lost everything, while I covered up my husband's emotional and physical problems, testing my faith in God beyond my wildest imagination.

I tried to get Jeff to tell this story for eight years. He would try so hard to write and then give up. I asked him to collaborate with me on this book and he declined. He did; however, preview and approve a proof copy of this book before it was published.

Brandi Winans

Will 1980 be the year for Jeff Winans?

Contents

Chapter 1

Broken Dreams

June 25, 2007, I boarded a plane to Washington D.C. to attend the Gridiron Greats Press Conference, June 26th, at the Washington Press Club and the NFL Congressional Hearings. While I was waiting for the plane to take off, I reached up, turned my air vent on, grabbed the airplane's blue blanket and snuggled up with my white airline pillow.

My mind wandered back to the month before when I was housesitting at my girlfriend's home and came upon a TV show called HBO's Real Sports with Bryant Gumbel. Bernie Goldberg was interviewing a young man named Chris Nowinski, author of Head Games: Football's Concussion Crisis, about his advocacy work raising awareness of the devastating consequences of sports concussions.

As Chris described the symptoms and long-term side effects of multiple concussions, a large knot in my stomach took me back to the deadly emotions over the years that had taken my marriage to a point of no return. I began to question if the emotional and behavioral problems that my former husband, Jeff, had been experiencing most of our married life were not what I thought they were, but possible after effects of his eleven-plus concussions from playing professional football. I needed to know more about these concussions, so I found Chris Nowinski on the internet and emailed him. Within twenty-four hours, he emailed me back and we set a time for a phone conversation a few days later.

The next morning while I was drinking my coffee and watching the local news on TV, I saw an interview with Mike Ditka. Mike was talking about the upcoming NFL congressional hearings in Washington D.C. and how the NFL wasn't paying players for their disabilities from injuries they sustained from playing professional football.

Until then, I had no idea how many other players had been turned down. Jeff and I fought the NFL for 16 years for his disability pension. But fighting for Jeff's NFL disability benefits was only a small part of everything we had been through during the last 25 years–including an horrific gunshot accident, the birth of our only son, having to file bankruptcy and losing everything–testing my faith in God in a way I could never imagined.

I knew that God never promised days without pain, laughter without sorrow or sun without rain. However, God did promise strength for the day, comfort for our tears and a light for the way. Sometimes it was hard to see the light through all of the tears.

Looking around the plane that morning I realized that everyone has a story to tell. Some stories are just bigger than others, but we all go through our own discoveries of life, experiencing the good, the bad and the ugly. Hopefully we grow and become better people because of it. This is the story of my life and marriage to former NFL Player Jeff Winans from 1978–2007.

In July 1978, after attending my 10th High School class reunion, I made a decision to move from Santa Monica, California back to Tampa Bay in Florida and open up a boutique. My current three-year marriage was very shaky after my husband, Rick, lost his ten-year job with Hanes Hosiery, and I thought if I moved home, the marriage could be saved.

My dreams of saving it were shattered when I found love letters in my husband's coat pocket from his mistress, as we were preparing to go up north to his father's house for Christmas. The envelopes revealed she had been writing him in care of general delivery at the local post office.

After confronting Rick and finding out the affair had been going on for over a year, we filed for divorce. Divorce came immediately, as there is no waiting period in Florida. Property settlement, however, took nine months. During that time my ex-husband and our new-found partner that we had brought on board to help finance the second store in Tampa, ousted me out of my corporation. By the time it was over, I was "broke and a joke."

Needing some extra income, I befriended a young gal named Patty from my apartment complex near the mall, where I had my boutique, and rented my extra bedroom to her.

My previous occupations had been colorful to say the least and included modeling, acting, business development and banking. I took a job as an account executive with a local talk radio station in the Tampa Bay area.

My older brother, Steve, was a senior producer/director for a local CBS affiliate. During the football season he would contract out with CBS in New York and work the Tampa Bay Buccaneers games. With his press passes, I was able to be on the sidelines and take photos. Through his connections, I started meeting a variety of new people, including an offensive lineman who played for the Bucs. Things seemed to be on the upswing and I was getting on with my life as a single gal.

There was another Tampa Bay Buc who visited my apartment complex, although he never noticed me. He would swirl into the parking lot in his 1976 white Cadillac El Dorado. Rumor was he was dating someone there. He was nice to look at, but in my opinion not available.

Jeffrey Dow Winans was tall, well built, and extremely handsome, reminding me of a Greek God with his curly black hair, deep brown eyes and a sculpted black beard. I later learned that he came from a small agricultural town in Northern California called Turlock, where melons, turkeys, nuts and wine were their major source of income. Blue Diamond Almonds and Gallo Winery's corporate offices were just up the street in Modesto. In the summer, the temperature would rise to a smoldering 110 degrees. In the winter months, it was known for its deadly fog.

During the summer, he worked in the melon fields for his father's best friend who distributed cantaloupes, honeydews and other melons all over the United States. His father, Glenn, had a local State Farm agency. Everyone knew everyone in Turlock.

As a country boy, Jeff excelled in sports, playing basketball, football and track at Turlock High School. Baseball was one of his real loves, but his coaches wouldn't let him play. After graduating from high school in 1969, he went to Modesto Junior College in Modesto, California, where he became the only six-letter winner in basketball and football. The college also claimed, in 1993, at his induction into their Hall of Fame, that he still held the record for the most unpaid parking tickets.

On the field and on the court, Jeff was relentless–giving and taking grueling hits to the head and body. In his second year at Modesto Junior College, his lifelong dream came true. He was offered a scholarship to USC in Southern California to play football for Coach John McKay.

His first year at USC was a real eye opener, especially coming from a small agricultural town. He struggled with his academics and the big city life. In his second year there he came to life on the field and was moved to first string.

Some of his teammates included: Pat Haden, Mike Rae, Anthony Davis, Lynn Swann, Sam "Bam" Cunningham, John Grant, Charles Young, Alan Graf, Steve Riley and Richard "Batman" Wood. They could jump and block like nothing anyone had ever seen. During a game against Notre Dame, Jeff was knocked out (his first concussion) and suffered a bruised sternum. That year, he received the 1972 "Most Improved Player" award from Coach McKay.

His USC football team went on to become National Champions, winning the Rose Bowl in 1973 against Ohio State. Jeff and his defensive line held them back. The team was recognized as one of the greatest college football teams of all times. Thirty three percent of the players were drafted to the pros. Jeff was one of them. Long time USC Alumnus William Block, author of An Immortal Team of Mortal Men, and sports writer Steve Travers (another fellow alumnus) has also written about the legendary football teams of USC.

As a second round draft pick (#32), Jeff was drafted by the Buffalo Bills. One of his Buffalo team members was Joe De Lamielleure. Joe would go on to be an NFL Hall of Famer years later. Heisman Trophy Winner, Hall of Famer and former USC alumni O.J. Simpson, known as "The Juice" had joined the team a few years before. In the 1973 season, O.J. went on to complete 2,000 rushing yards. The offensive line was known as the "Electric Company."

Jeff started nine games in 1973 as defensive tackle. The offensive and defensive linemen are the unknown soldiers and are always getting banged up. They hit hard and are hit hard. They bang heads. Unless you are knocked out, some concussions are simply considered headaches.

The following year at Buffalo, Jeff suffered a torn ACL to the knee and sat out all of 1974 on injured reserve. He came back in 1975 and played eleven games. In 1976, Jeff was traded twice, first to the New Orleans Saints where he played only three games, and second to the Oakland Raiders with Coach John Madden. At that time, Madden decided to move him to offensive guard.

During his time at USC, Jeff met his first wife, Laurie, and they married in 1976. They rented an apartment in San Mateo with their Saint Bernard named Bernie and took up housekeeping. The time with the Raiders was also short- lived. Without warning, he was traded to a new expansion team called the Tampa Bay Buccaneers in Tampa, Florida, where he signed a six-year contract. He later learned that the trades were done to prevent him from being picked up by the Dallas Cowboys.

Jeff fit in well at Tampa and McKay (his former USC Coach), kept him at offensive guard. December 12, 1977, after being 0-26, the Bucs won their first game against New Orleans. Jeff was back on his game. This, too, was to be short-lived. In 1978 he sustained major back, neck and more head injuries–forcing him to sit out the rest of the season.

Within a year after Jeff's move to Tampa, his three-year marriage to Laurie was over. She moved into an apartment and Jeff stayed in the house they had bought together until it was sold. Some of Jeff's friends from Buffalo who worked at a local Clearwater bar rented rooms from him. While he was at Buffalo, he and a couple of other players ventured into the bar business, which brings me back to how we first met.

Patty, my new roomy had been asking me to go to a local bar called Molly Maguire's near our apartment. It wasn't my cup of tea. It attracted mainly a younger crowd (Patty was 19 and the drinking age was 18) but to get her off my back, I looked over at her one night and said, "Okay Patty, it's now or never."

She looked at me with a puzzled look on her face, "Now or never for what?"

"You've been asking me to go to Molly Maguire's with you, so let's go now."

"It's only eight o'clock."

"I know, so are we going or what?" I jokingly asked.

I was heading over to Tampa later to meet some friends and decided to make a quick stop at Molly Maguire's. Patty got up out of the rocker and threw on some other clothes.

When we got to the bar, no one was there except me, Patty, the bartender, and this Greek God I saw at my apartment complex all the time. He was sitting at the bar in a pair of jeans and a grey tank top. His neck, forearms, shoulder and back muscles made it obvious that he was an athlete. As we walked up behind him, he turned around, smiled at Patty, who he knew from the pool, and said, "Hey, Patty, who's your friend?"

"This is Brandi my new roomy. Brandi, this is Jeff Winans."

"Hello Brandi, Patty told me she had a roommate. Are you the one who owned the store in the Clearwater Mall?"

"Yeah, I had a boutique but I lost it in my divorce. I work for a radio station now."

"Can I buy you a drink?"

"Sure, thanks."

He pulled back the bar stool as I sat down. He had a gorgeous smile, tanned face, dark curly hair and brown eyes that you could get lost in. He was easy to talk to and I couldn't take my eyes off of him. The next hour went by fast.

"So Brandi, how about going out with me sometime," he asked in a flirtatious way.

He could see that he caught me completely off guard.

"Maybe sometime", I replied as I looked back into his eyes with a flirtatious smile of my own.

It killed me to say that, because there was a very strong physical attraction, something I hadn't felt for a long time and it scared me. He looked at me with his eyebrows raised and just shook his head with a smirk that stared a hole through me. I don't think many girls had ever blown him off before.

"Brandi, it was nice meeting you. I'll see you around sometime."

He stood up, walked down to the end of the bar and started talking to some other people he knew. I stood up, looked over at him, smiled and left to meet my friends in Tampa. I soon found myself going to Molly Maguire's more often than I should have.

Chapter 2

Moving On

The next few months flew by. Work at the radio station was going well. I was going out with another other Buccaneer and a guy I met from Atlanta while he was vacationing. We had a lot of fun together, no serious romance. I wasn't ready for that yet. Plus I was fighting something that would soon overtake me. I couldn't get Jeff Winans out of my head.

Patty spent a lot of time at the apartment pool and always kept me up on the local buzz. She came in one day and said, "I heard that Jeff's divorce is final. Have you thought anymore about going out with him?"

"Is he still seeing the girl who lives here?" She didn't know that he was constantly on my mind.

"You mean Sally?" she said, questioning why I would care.

"Yes".

"Why would that keep you from going out with him?"

"I don't know. I don't want to go out with him if he is seeing someone else. Plus, I live here and so does she."

"Well you're seeing a couple of guys. But Brandi, every time I see him, he asks about you. If you don't go out with him, maybe I will," she said as she plopped into the rocking chair.

I looked at her dumfounded. "I thought you were engaged to some guy up north?"

"I am, but he's not a Tampa Bay Buccaneer and you know what a groupie I am. Ha."

"Yeah, yeah; if he asks me out again, I'll go."

A few nights later, I was in bed asleep when I heard some commotion in the living room, and then Patty walked in my bedroom all excited.

"Brandi, are you awake?" I could tell by her slurred voice she was not feeling any pain.

"Patty, I said sharply, what time is it?"

"I don't know, but guess who I brought home?"

"Who"? I said, uninterested.

"Wino."

I sat up in the bed. "You mean Jeff Winans?"

"Yes", she said laughing. "He's too drunk to drive, so I told him he could stay here. See you in the morning."

I was wide awake and my heart was pounding as she slid off my bed, walked out and closed the bedroom door. I couldn't stand it. I waited a minute, got out of my bed, tiptoed over and put my ear up to my bedroom door.

I heard laughing, then a few minutes later, silence. I had to know what they were doing so I opened my door, got down on my belly and slowly crawled down the hall to her bedroom. The thought of them doing anything was driving me crazy, so I put my ear to her door and listened for about fifteen seconds. I wasn't sure what I was going to do but I was determined to interrupt them. That's when I carefully opened the door and peeked in.

Patty was on her bed asleep and Jeff was lying on the floor snoring. I was so relieved. A peace came over me and I realized how much I really liked this man. In other words, if he asked me out again, I knew I would go.

After giving the ex-wife everything, Jeff was relying on his salary to get him through the season and back on his feet financially. He was in full form at the training camp in July, 1979. But in August 1979, he was injured in an exhibition game and broke his foot. Then came something he had not expected to happen–he was waived. He said it was because he wouldn't go out and play with a cast on his foot. At that time, I had no idea how the NFL worked.

After being waived by the Tampa Bay Bucs, Jeff filed a grievance with the NFL Players Union. The Players Association rep told Jeff that he had no recourse over the Bucs waiving him and that he should sit out, get healed, decide on some teams that he wanted to play for and write to them. In other words, don't rock the boat and do as you are told if you want to play again in the NFL. Create problems for us and we'll create problems for you.

Jeff was devastated. He thought he had a case against the Bucs because of the way they released him. With a lot of free time on his hands, we started hanging out more. One day I asked him about Sally. I needed to know where they stood. He seemed surprised that I knew about her.

"There's nothing between Sally and me except sex, and she's more for convenience."

"Why do you care so much since you won't officially go out with me? Come on," he said with those gorgeous eyes and smile, "what do you have to lose? We might have a good time."

I dropped my guard, and looked directly at him with a seductive smile, "All right, I'll go out with you on a few dates, and see where that goes, but I'm not going to jump in the sack with you".

"We'll see," he said, flashing that flirtatious smile.

A few dates turned into–a lot of dates. We always had fun together. There were times, however, when I could see he was in a great deal of pain, with his pride trying to cover it up. Sometimes it would overtake him and he would take whatever he could get his hands on to make it go away.

Labor Day 1979, the Maguire brothers had a big party at Molly Maguire's. Jeff's sister, Sandra, was in town from San Diego. We had spoken on the phone before, but we had never met. We hit it off immediately.

She saw how close Jeff and I had become and confided in me that her parents had sent her because they were worried about him, especially since the divorce. I started seeing a pattern, but I couldn't help myself. I was falling in love with him.

All of my life, I had been a rescuer of some sort. I rescued all the animals in the neighborhood. I took care of my friends as if they were family.

My grandfather Grayson (Papa) died of a heart attack when I was twelve. My father died two years later of lung cancer. They were the two greatest influences on me at that time in my life. We moved from Southern California after Dad suffered a severe Heart attack when I was six years old had to retire from the Marine Corp. The doctors said Florida would be better for his health. After the move, he graduated from a local business college and got a job as the General Manager at one of the beach hotels.

They didn't know that much about lung cancer back then. They cut him from one clavicle to the other and then removed the lung from the side. The radiation was horrible. I watched his skin burned to a deep red, as paralysis set in on his right side.

It was so painful to watch him from across the dinner table at night as he would take his left hand and hold his right hand to feed himself. None of us could say anything. It would take away his dignity. It was who he was; once a Marine, always a Marine. That's the way we had been taught–to be warriors, be tough, be strong, but with heart and integrity.

The day he had to go back into the hospital, he came over and sat down at the dining room table while I was eating breakfast. He had his favorite white hat on, was wearing a blue Hawaiian shirt with green palm trees and a pair of white shorts. He was so thin. As I looked up at him, tears were rolling down his face.

"Brandi, I don't want to go back to the hospital. I want to stay here. I know that I don't have much time left but your Mom and the doctors are insisting."

I took a deep breath, stood up and put my arms around him. It was everything I could do to hold back my tears. I didn't want him to know how much I was hurting inside.

"Everything's going to be okay, Dad, and I will always be your little girl."

They flew him to Walter Reed Hospital in Washington, D.C. to be operated on again November, 1963, a few days before President

Kennedy was assassinated. He and my mother watched the President's funeral procession from his hospital room. Dad died February 13, 1964. His death and funeral was one of the hardest things I had to go through in my almost fourteen years. He was buried with full military honors and a twenty-one-gun salute.

My mother, bless her heart, was already very unstable and had tried to commit suicide a few years before. By the age of fifteen, I was taking care of her. By the time I was eighteen, we had sold the house, lost pretty much everything and I was California bound to follow my dreams.

What was I going to do about my Prince Charming? Was I his rescuer or was he mine?

Chapter 3

Partners in Pain

One of the things that Jeff and I had in common was the fact that we were both animal lovers. Jeff took Bernie his St. Bernard, when he and Laurie divorced. Since dogs were not allowed at the regular beaches, Jeff would borrow one of his roommate's cars and we would take Bernie over to the local Courtney Campbell Causeway beach so he could go swimming. On one occasion, Mike, another bartender friend of Jeff's and Patty joined us. We had a great afternoon, swimming and playing Frisbee.

On the way home, we were involved in a severe automobile accident, which forced us to rear-end a car at 60 miles per hour. Seat belts weren't required to be worn then. I woke up lying on the grass by the car. I don't know if I was thrown out due to the impact or if I was taken and placed there. I could see flashing lights and the next thing I remember I was waking up in the ambulance in a lot of pain.

After the x-rays and CAT scan at the hospital, I found out how lucky I was. I had a hairline fracture on my frontal skull between my eyebrows, and severe neck trauma along with a major concussion. I looked like a "cone head" from Saturday Night Live. Patty had broken her nose on the dash. We were all very lucky to be alive. Jeff had stayed behind with Bernie.

When I was able to leave the hospital, Jeff took me home to his house. Because of the fracture and concussion, I had to keep my head in a certain position. It was very difficult getting around–even to go to the bathroom. I would get very dizzy and nauseous. At times, everything was foggy; I had no short-term memory and a constant headache.

A few days after I came home, Jeff shook my shoulder in the middle of the night, "Brandi wake up, I don't feel well."

I turned over and looked at him. His body shook from chills and sweat poured from his face. I touched his forehead. He was burning up with fever. I thought he had a bout of the flu. Then I felt something wet under the sheets.

I turned the night stand lamp on and pulled the sheet back to see what was going on. It wasn't sweat—it was blood. There was a distinctive red line going from his leg, hip and up to his waist. I knew what that meant. When I was ten years old, my grandfather had blood poisoning and almost died. Jeff never told anyone he'd been injured in the accident.

I knew I had to get him to the emergency room (it was before 911) and I started praying for God to help me. There was a hospital close by so I decided to go for it. I was dizzy and I could hardly stand up as I got out of bed. At first, I wasn't sure if I could do it, but Jeff needed me.

"Honey, put your arm around me. We have to get you to the hospital".

He turned his head toward me and saw the urgency in my face. Somehow, I got him out of the bed and we made it down the stairs and into the car. I was so nauseous I thought I was going to throw up as I broke out in my own sweat, but I knew I had to get us there in one piece.

I started the car, turned my head and slowly backed out of the driveway. I had to drive with my head slightly tilted back so I wouldn't get dizzy. A few minutes later, I pulled up to the emergency doors of the hospital and started honking the horn and screaming for help. I leaned my head back on the headrest and said, "Thank you Jesus."

One of the ER staff and a security guard came out to see what was going on. They got Jeff out of the car and placed him on a gurney. Two other ER staff helped me out of the car, where I threw up at the entrance doors and collapsed. The hospital ER room was very busy.

Thirty minutes later, I was feeling better. The orange juice and lying down seemed to work for now. I insisted they give my bed to some else and they escorted me to Jeff's room, where he was waiting for the Bucs Physician to arrive. The ER doctor had already given him the assessment over the phone and we didn't want any media attention. I sat down in the lounge chair and waited with Jeff. Upon his arrival, he told us that he needed to get Jeff admitted so he could get him into surgery and cut out the infection.

Jeff immediately said, "No way Doc." Do what you need to do, but I'm not staying!" You didn't argue with him when he was in that kind of emotional distress. They gave him a local.

I watched Jeff as he endured the pain and was amazed at how much pain he could tolerate. I realized that being able to sustain pain was part of the game of football. I thought I would cringe as the doctor cut out the infection. But, to my surprise, I found it fascinating. Maybe it was because I had worked as a nurse's aide in high school, or maybe as long as it wasn't my blood I was all right. The hospital incident brought us even closer and made both of us realize how much we cared for one another.

A few nights later, he said, "B (his nickname for me), I have very strong feelings for you. I have to be out of this house soon. I know you have your place in Clearwater, but I want to be with you and I would like you to think about getting a place together and moving in with me. I don't know if I'm going to be picked up by another team. If I do get picked up by another team, I want you to go with me. I know it's a lot to think about."

He took me by surprise. My mind was racing, looking for the right words to come out. "I love being with you, too, but you're right–it is a lot to think about. We've both made a lot of changes over the last year and I really need some time to think about it."

A few weeks later, I decided to follow my heart and go for it. Jeff was on the mend and I was feeling better except for the problems with my memory. I was still having trouble concentrating. I could read a paragraph in the newspaper and a minute later, I couldn't tell you what I read. It was extremely frustrating. My doctor decided to send me to see a neurologist in Clearwater. After a thorough examination he said, "Brandi, concussions can create a number of physical problems. Memory is only one of them. I'm going to put you on a drug called Ametriphfolene. It should help you to focus, regain your short-term memory and allow you to be able to regain your concentration. As you progress we will increase the dosage."

"How long will I have to be on this?"

"Everyone is different." We'll see how you are doing in a month and reevaluate at that time."

One of the teams Jeff wanted to play for again was the Oakland Raiders. He liked Coach Madden when he was there in 1976 and there was a history with Al Davis, who was still managing owner of the Raiders. So that was the team he decided to pursue.

A month later, the Raiders phoned and picked him up. It was nice to see him so excited. He would head out in a few months and his Dad would fly out from Turlock to make the ride back with him. I was looking forward to meeting his Dad. I decided to stay in Tampa until he got out there and settled in. For now he needed to concentrate on healing and playing football.

The next year flew by. I left the Radio station after being offered a job as a Sales Manager for a Cable TV station in Largo. On the weekends, I worked the football games with my brother, Steve. So I was on the sidelines a lot. It was a fun time. We hung out with some of the other players and their girlfriends. In 1979 the Bucs made history, winning their first NFC Central Championship.

Jeff was doing great in Oakland. He was rooming with John Matusak (Tooz). They rented a condo in Alameda near the Raiders training camp. Once a month I made a care package: chocolate chip cookies, brownies, a few other treats, and would send it to Jeff and Tooz. I talked to Jeff's mom and dad frequently and planned a trip out in October to go to a Raiders' game and finally meet his mom. But, in September 1980, he was hit during a game against New England. He took a cheap shot from another player and crushed his ankle.

The Raiders flew him to Cedar Sinai Hospital in Los Angeles for emergency surgery. I wanted to fly to Los Angeles to be with him, but he insisted I wait until he returned to Oakland and was a little more stable. He would not be returning that season. In order to play for Oakland after he left Tampa Bay, he had to waive his claim to any future back injuries (which we later learned was illegal).

I flew out to Oakland a few weeks later. He was recuperating well and he insisted on picking me up at the airport. Because of his masculine size and dark curly hair, he was easy to spot at the airport baggage claim. He had a large walking cast on his left leg, but a big smile on his face. As we embraced and kissed he said, "I'm glad you're here. I've really missed you". That was all I needed to hear.

"I've missed you too honey." I melted into his arms.

Just after leaving the airport, we passed Tooz on the road. He was taking one of his girlfriends back to the airport and honked as he drove by us. The Alameda townhouse Jeff and Tooz were renting during the season was a two story with high ceilings and sliding glass doors that went out to a nice wood patio area and a large Jacuzzi.

We had some nice private time until Tooz came home about an hour later. He came in the door calling out our names like a little kid looking for his parents. Jeff's bedroom had a little window with shutters that you could open up and look down into the living room. Tooz loved to play disc jockey, so he put on some of his oldies but goodies records and started singing and carrying on.

"Jeff, Jeff, Brandi, come downstairs. I don't have anyone to play with. Please."

Tooz was so funny and quite the character. He always carried a sword and a Colt 45 handgun in the front seat of his Lincoln Continental. He had developed a reputation for being a little in "Left" field. Jeff was always telling me funny stories of himself, Hendricks and Tooz, and told me how guys would pick on them because they were so big.

Jeff said it was always the little guys who felt they had to prove something, and it seemed like Tooz was always being sued.

As an actor, Tooz had already made several movies, and at 6'8" he made Jeff, who was 6'5 1/2", look small. Tooz played in the movies "Cave Man" and "North Dallas Forty" which was a lot like the real Tooz.

"North Dallas Forty" showed the very political side of football and was one of my favorite movies. I saw similar situations that Jeff was living everyday and compared him to Nick Nolte's character.

We had a great time in Alameda and a few days later we drove to Turlock to see Jeff's Mom and Dad. He didn't feel comfortable staying at his parent's home. I understood and respected that so we stayed at the only hotel in his hometown called "The Gardens".

He had not been himself the morning we were going to visit his parents. He was nervous and jittery. As we were getting ready to leave the hotel, he grabbed my hand and blurted out, "Brandi, whatever happens today, don't let my mother make you cry."

The look on his face showed me he was very serious.

"Why would you say that?"

"Because every girl I ever brought home, she made cry."

"Honey either your mom is going to like me or she's not, but I promise you, she won't make me cry, okay?"

"But…"

I put my fingertips on his lips. He looked at me with that little boy look,

"Okay."

We pulled in his parent's driveway. It was a beautiful traditional home and looked like something out of Better Homes and Gardens magazine. Fall was in the air, and we sat outside by the pool on their brick patio that Glenn and Jeff had laid many years before.

We had a wonderful visit and got along great. It was my last visit to California that year and I decided to move there after this football season was over.

The Mayflower Van pulled out of the driveway. As I looked through the house for the last time, it seemed like only yesterday we had rented it.

My brother Steve offered to let Bernie, ShayJay (my cat) and me stay with him until Jeff was able to get back from the playoffs. The Oakland Raiders had made a huge comeback and were now in the playoffs. Jeff was placed on injured reserve and was out for the season. Super Bowl XV was in New Orleans and if they made it through the playoffs, it wouldn't be that far to travel.

Christmas came and Mom had cooked a fabulous Christmas dinner at Steve's house in Parkland Estates. Jeff and I celebrated Christmas over the phone. Before I knew it, New Years Eve was here and 1980 was over.

The Raiders were unstoppable in the playoffs. Now, a dream come true, they would be a part of history in Super Bowl XV in New Orleans against the Philadelphia Eagles. This was what every player works for and dreams of every day. I was so excited for Jeff and his teammates.

Because he was on injured reserve, Jeff wasn't allowed to travel with the team. The coaches didn't like the injured players to be around the players who are healthy, so he would be coming home before the game and we would be able to go together.

Without warning, Bernie, Jeff's St. Bernard took ill. The vet said it didn't look good, so I decided to call Jeff. He called me back a few hours later and he was able to get a flight home the next day. He said that the Raiders would overnight us tickets to the game and send them to Steve's house. All I could do now was pray for Bernie to hang on until Jeff got home.

I picked him up at the Tampa International Airport the next afternoon. I could see the stress in his face over Bernie, so I took him directly to the vet. The prayers and medication they were giving Bernie were working, and if all stayed well he would be able to go home the following day. We were both so relieved. Now we could concentrate on going to New Orleans. I grilled some steaks and made a fabulous homecoming dinner. Steve and his girlfriend Kathy joined us.

The next afternoon, Bernie was ready to go home and I picked him up from the Vet after work. He was his old self and anxious to leave–dragging me out of the vet's office and jumping into the front seat of my car.

It was cold outside and my brother, who was low on cash again, had not bought fuel oil to heat the house. Jeff decided to cut down one of the trees in Steve's back yard for firewood and use the fireplace in the living room to heat the house.

As we pulled into Steve's driveway, Bernie whined to get out, then ran to the back door and whined some more. As I opened the back door, I saw Jeff with his shirt off, muscles flexed, sweat pouring off his body, chopping down one of Steve's large oak trees using nothing more than a hatchet. Bernie ran over to him and almost knocked him off his feet. He was glad to see Bernie but was concentrating on the oak tree, determined to chop and make firewood.

He turned around and gave me a dorky smile. I could see that he was feeling no pain. My brother came out of the house and we all started laughing at Jeff trying to chop this tree down with a hatchet.

When Jeff tried to light a fire in the fireplace, we realized that the firewood that he had chopped up was too green and unseasoned to burn. To keep all of us warm, I went out and bought thermal heating blankets. It looked pretty funny, with all of us walking around in blankets with cords trailing behind us, and it was nice to have some laughter in the house. The next morning, I started getting our clothes ready for the trip to New Orleans.

"Did our plane tickets and hotel info arrive?" Jeff asked.

"Not yet", I replied.

He called the Raiders office again and they kept insisting they had sent them over-night. He asked them to track them and call him back.

"Are we going to have to drive?" I asked.

He didn't reply but the look on his face and his body language said it all. He was hurt and angry all at the same time. The NFL gives each active player four Super Bowl Tickets, and two of Jeff's buddies from Buffalo were supposed to go with us. I could see he was becoming more distraught. A few minutes later, he just blew up. His body was shaking; his face was purple-red.

He turned around in the kitchen and stormed out. I could hear him talking to his friends who we were going with and telling them to just come by and pick up their tickets.

His stubborn dogmatic streak came out and we never made it to New Orleans. The Raiders beat the Eagles and we had missed a once in a lifetime moment to celebrate with the team. Jeff had every reason to celebrate. He was a part of the team and part of football history. His injuries mattered. He didn't see it that way. He had missed the greatest moment in his life and all he had in him at that point was anger, a pity party, and a bottle of pain pills.

Part of me understood and part of me didn't know what to do. I knew he was distraught over the way the Raiders had treated him. There was no consoling him. I had to give him his space, let it pass and let him deal with it.

April 1981, we were California bound.

Chapter 4

California, Here We Come

Jeff had been working hard getting ready for the Raiders mini-camp in May 1981. The formal Super Bowl XV ring ceremony was in August before the first exhibition game in Oakland. It takes that long for all the rings to be made as each one is customized with their name and number. He and Tooz were rooming together again in Alameda, where the Raiders training camp was located.

Modesto is a very quaint community about twenty-five minutes north of Turlock. We found a beautiful home on the outskirts of Modesto about an hour from Alameda. Modesto was also the hometown of George Lucas, the creator of Star Wars, and downtown Turlock was where they shot some of the film for American Graffiti.

It was nice to see the Mayflower Van after so many months of living out of a suitcase. I had a lot to get used in the Central Valley. It was the first time I had ever been away from the water. The Sierra Nevada Mountains were less than two hours away, as was a big lake called Pine Crest. Jeff's parents had a large Winnebago motor home and traveled there quite extensively. One of their favorite spots was a campground by the lake.

The Raiders Mini Camp in May of 1981 took a toll on Jeff.. He came home five days later and the only place he wasn't black and blue were a few places on his face. Welcome to the NFL. This time his body seemed to take forever to heal. He was always prone to infections and he was still having trouble with his ankle and his back. But he was determined to make the team and prove himself once more.

The regular NFL Raider Camp got under way in July in Alameda. He had been there a few days, when I got the call. He started off with small talk then his voice became very emotional, shaky, cracking.

"Honey, what's wrong?"

"I had my physical today."

"How did you do?" I asked wanting to know, but not wanting to know.

"Not so well, they want me to waive my ankle in order to sign a new contract." He had already waived his back to play the year before.

"How do you feel about that?" There was a moment of silence. "Honey, are you there?"

"Yes, I'm here," he said in a small child-like emotional tone. "For the first time in my life, I'm afraid to go on the field".

I closed my eyes. I could feel his pain. "Then maybe it's time to come home."

"I waived my back last year," he said, his voice cracking.

"I know honey; you're the only one who can make this decision. Whatever you decide, I'm here for you. I love you and we'll get through this together."

"I love you too. I have a lot to think about."

I hung up the phone and prayed.

I wasn't sure what he would decide, but the next day I decided to make his favorite cheese casserole. I could always freeze it for another time if he decided to stay at camp. I was just putting it in the oven when I heard the garage door open.

He had made his decision to come home. He pulled in the garage. I heard his car door open and close, and stood there anticipating the walk through the door. I was standing by the oven and looked over at him. He looked at me, walked over, put his arms around me and we just held each other.

No words were needed. He needed me and I was there. I needed him and he was there. With God's help, we would get through this. This was a major turning point in his life. The only career he'd ever known was over. He was thirty years old.

Once you are waived by the NFL—your salary ends. It doesn't matter how many years are left on your contract. Jeff's money had ended last season, and it wouldn't be long before our savings would be gone.

He called the NFL Player's rep to file a grievance and we were assigned an NFL attorney out of Oakland named Wayne Hooper. He was supposed to help us file for total and permanent disability and workers compensation.

I knew I needed to find a job and since my first love had always been acting, I answered an ad in the local Modesto paper looking for several Cable TV hosts for a weekly show called, "Sunday Brunch". The producer was Dustin Costa.

All the local talent showed up including a local radio announcer, Bob Williams. A few days later, I got a call. I had been cast as one of the hosts for the restaurant, movie reviews and community affairs segment. I would co-host with a fitness expert, Linda Roman, and the local radio announcer, Bob Williams. It was a packed two hours.

However, it was a small cable TV station. No editing equipment–which meant we had to do multiple takes until we got one right. It was like filming in the Stone Age. We would shoot during the week in-house and on location, and the show would run on Sunday mornings from nine to eleven.

It felt good to be working. Jeff really needed some space to think about what he was going to do with the rest of his life. His ankle and back were a constant problem and he spent most of his days on the floor with his legs elevated on a pillow. Although I tried to understand what he was going through, his mood swings were becoming more dominant and intimidating. Dustin, my producer, called one day. "Has Jeff decided what he wants to do?"

"No. His back and ankles are a constant problem for him and he's filed a grievance with the Players Union."

"Would he like to do a sports segment on the show?"

"I don't know. Why don't you give him a call?"

Jeff seemed to perk up when we talked more about it that night and decided to see if he could do it. He did really well for his television debut but, unfortunately, it was too much for his body. After three shows, he had to quit.

Soon the producer's money ran out and Sunday Brunch was over. It was fun while it lasted and been a great experience; something that could go on my resume.

We had heard nothing from the NFL and with Jeff's frustration, the tension between us continued to build. With our savings very low, I needed to find another job.

I found an ad in the classifieds for an outside sales rep with a nationwide insurance replacement company. It was a great job opportunity with lots of perks and benefits, but I would have to work out of four offices: Modesto, Stockton, San Jose and Bakersfield.

The pay included a base salary, bonuses from all four offices, a new company car, car insurance, expense account and medical benefits. Having a company car meant that Jeff wouldn't be without transportation while I was gone.

The job wasn't where my heart was, but it would put food on the table. The bad part was that I would be on the road a lot.

The Super Bowl XV Ring Ceremony that August came and went. Jeff was never notified and was very angry and hurt when he read about it in the paper. Besides the love of the game, the ring is what the players play for, and very few ever get one.

He had a long-standing relationship with owner Al Davis since his USC days. When he called the Raiders about it, they said that Al Davis changed his mind about giving him a ring because Jeff chose not to sign the new contract. Now, Al wouldn't even return any of his phone calls. The last thing he had said to Jeff when his ankle was crushed during the season game was, "You really disappointed me, Jeff."

Football had been Jeff's life since before high school. He had put his trust in the NFL. He played seven years and was vested for a pension after five years. He was injured on the job and became totally disabled and unable to work. He remembered that the NFL always told him that "we take care of our own".

After what Al Davis did regarding the Super Bowl Ring and the way he been treated, it was the last straw for Jeff. A friend of his referred us to an attorney in San Diego and we filed a lawsuit against the Oakland Raiders for 12 million dollars. The attorney also told us that Jeff might qualify for Social Security Disability, so I filed the paperwork. These were two separate cases that had nothing to do with each other.

Since Hooper had been appointed by the NFL, Jeff put all of his confidence into him to fight and represent us well to get worker's comp while we were waiting on his Total and Permanent Disability. Hooper said all along that this was going to be a long process that it had to be done in a certain order. He told us to be patient. Patience was something Jeff had very little of, but he seemed to have his fight back.

I thought this could be something that could occupy his time and give him hope. He had kept a relationship with one of the coaches at Modesto Junior College, and knowing his situation, they offered him a coaching job.

Excitement turned to disappointment once again when he found that his body wouldn't hold up. In his mind he had too much pride to just stand on the sidelines and feel like a dilapidated old man. He quit three days later. Every time he started to feel worthy or useful, disappointment seemed to follow. It killed me to see him like that, because I knew how much he wanted to work and provide for his family.

One thing he started to enjoy was cooking. He could do it at home at his own pace and he soon became a fabulous cook. He developed a caramel corn recipe. Whenever he knew I was coming home, he would make dinner for me. One particular night I was exhausted and it was a wonderful surprise. There were lit candles on the dining room table. I walked over to him and gave him a very gentle kiss.

"This so special honey; I really needed this today, Thank you."

"You deserve it. You've been working so hard."

After we sat down, he looked at me with a big smile, "Guess what? I was able to get us tickets to see Smokey Robinson in Reno".

We both loved Smokey. "You're kidding, when?"

"December 18. My friend Paul and his wife Luisa will be going with us. I booked us a reservation at the new MGM Grand Hotel. We're going to have a great time."

"Oh honey, I can't wait. It will be so nice to get away. I'll make sure I can get off. I reached over and gave him another kiss. I touched his tender lips and melted. My body ached for him. We hadn't made love in a while, but tonight all of our troubles disappeared.

We flew to Reno the morning of the 18th. It was the first time we had been away together since Jeff played football. Paul's fear of flying got the best of him, so he and Luisa made the four hour drive by car and met us there. The airplane ride was bumpy but the view was spectacular.

Our room was gorgeous, with a large suite and a balcony with a view of the snow-capped mountains. There was a huge round bed with a navy blue velvet bedspread with gold trim, matching drapes and a Jacuzzi tub in the bathroom.

We decided to go shopping while we were waiting for Paul and Luisa to arrive. The two of us were like little kids in a candy store, buying some crazy hats and toys.

Paul and Luisa arrived about an hour after we did. They joined us on the bottom floor of the hotel where the MGM Lion was on display. After a few hours of browsing around and visiting, we went back to the room to get dressed for dinner.

I couldn't get over the change in Jeff. He was so playful, hugging, touching. I walked in the bathroom to brush my teeth. He followed, pulled me close and started to caress my neck. I turned around took his hand, gazed into his eyes and slowly walked out of the bathroom to the bed. He picked me up, threw me on the bed and I bounced like a trampoline when he jumped on the bed next to me.

We couldn't stop laughing. Jeff looked at me so tenderly, like I was a fragile piece of crystal. Soon our passion ran deep and we made love. After, we just held each other. I never felt so much like I was Cinderella and Jeff was Prince Charming.

Before we knew it, it was time to get dressed for Smokey Robinson. Jeff looked so handsome in his three-piece suit. I had never seen him dressed up before. I had on a halter style slinky black dress with a low back.

We met Paul and Luisa at the entrance of the dinner theater. Inside were large elevated tables, half-booth style, and center stage. I don't think there was a bad seat in the house. While dinner was being served, I noticed some people that we knew at another table and waived to them.

"Honey, look, there's Mike and Brenda."

He looked at me with a big smile on his face, "I know".

"Oh, did Paul invite them?

"No, I did."

"You did? Why?"

"So they can help us celebrate.

"Celebrate what?"

"Celebrate us getting married tomorrow."

I looked at him with eyes as big as saucers. "What did you say? I thought you said that we were getting married tomorrow?"

"That's what I said. Paul and Luisa are going to stand up for us. I wanted to surprise you".

There was no, "I love you and want to spend the rest of my life with you." There was no "Will you marry me?" It was simply, "We're getting married in the morning, Paul and Luisa are standing up for us, and the rest of the group is here to be a part of the wedding party."

I stared at him in disbelief. When he saw the look on my face, he looked at me a little distraught, "I thought this was what you wanted?"

I remembered the argument a few months before when I had mentioned getting married and having a family and how upset he had gotten because he didn't know what would be happening with his career or how he would be able to provide for us. Now three months later everything had changed. I couldn't help but wonder why.

I was speechless (which is rare for me). It was what I wanted, but it wasn't how I envisioned getting married. My Prince Charming would take me out for a romantic dinner, get on his knees, hand me a ring and ask me to be his wife. Maybe I had seen too many fairy tale movies.

I looked at him, smiled and gave him a soft kiss on his mouth and said quietly, "This is the best surprise I could have ever imagined. Yes, I'll marry you."

The next thing I heard was "Ladies and Gentlemen, Smokey Robinson." Smokey gave one of the best performances I have ever seen. After the show we went gambling, had a few drinks, and I got to know the people who were going to stand up for us.

The nine o'clock morning wake-up call came too soon. The ceremony was scheduled at The Chapel of the Bells at eleven. Jeff had thought of everything except a ring. He said we would pick one out after we got home, so for now I went into the gift shop and bought a cheap costume one that I could slip on for show.

A 1956 Cadillac limo picked us up at the hotel at ten thirty. Outside it was cold, wet and starting to snow. Reality was starting to set in and I was a nervous wreck. Did I really want to marry this man? Look at all the trouble he went to–but look at all the hell we had been through since we had been together. I knew he loved me. I knew I loved him more than life itself and that's what scared me the most, but I had wanted more than anything was to be his wife and have a family. Then more second thoughts. I started to sweat. It was thirty degrees outside and I was sweating; so was Jeff. What was he feeling? Was he having second thoughts?

I hardly remember the ceremony. My heart was racing. The minister was saying "Do you take this man to be your lawful wedded husband, to love honor and cherish?" When it came time to slip the ring on my finger, it wouldn't go on. Jeff kept trying to push it on. Then he grabbed my hand and wet my finger with his mouth. I was so embarrassed. Finally, he slipped it on my pinkie and said, "With this ring I thee wed."

Everyone laughed and a peace came over me that I can't explain. I looked into Jeff's eyes and smiled that girlish smile; "Yes I take this man to be my lawful wedded husband."

I got married in a pair of wool slacks and a white ruffled taffeta blouse. Jeff got married in a pair of blue jeans, a plaid shirt and a tan blazer. So much for tradition. Paul and Luisa threw rice on us as we got in the limo and went back to the hotel.

I came to Reno for the Smokey Robinson concert, and on December 19, 1981, I ended up as Mrs. Jeff Winans. It was a wonderful weekend and I finally felt like this was going to be a positive turning point in our lives.

Chapter 5

Moving Forward

We were settling into life as a married couple and struggling to move forward with the NFL stuff. Jeff was expecting things to go smoothly, but not much was happening on the disability case with Wayne Hooper. Hooper told us he was waiting for the NFL to appoint a neutral physician in our area. (The neutral physician determines whether or not you are disabled from football). I was getting the feeling that Hooper didn't know what he was doing.

Jeff had a hard time handling disappointment. He acted like a little kid whose mother had taken the candy away from him, and he would pout. His headaches were a constant problem and I was starting to see changes in his memory. He would forget things, get disoriented and confused. I assumed it was from the amount of prescriptions he was taking for his physical problems never thinking it might be something else.

By July 1982, he got more and more lost inside himself and things started taking a horrible turn for the worse as his depression, started affecting everything. He would feed off my strength alienating everyone and go into his own little world. He had a hard time sleeping so he would stay up most of the night. A pattern started. He would get up late-morning, smoke a joint, pop some pills, open a liter of Diet Coke and read the entire paper. By the time he read half of the paper, he was feeling no pain.

His headaches became more frequent and more severe as his

physical body was deteriorating. He said the pot helped his head-aches and pain. I didn't do drugs, so it was hard for me to under-stand.

I also didn't realize at the time that I was becoming such an en-abler, trying to justify his behavior in my own mind and then com-ing up behind him and picking up the pieces. I felt responsible for his well-being and I loved him so much I didn't know what else to do. There were days that, in his eyes, I could do nothing right. It was a "catch 22" for both of us.

We needed some extra funds, so we filed for Jeff's 25% early retire-ment. It wasn't what he hoped for and only amounted to $6,107.00. I continued to work.

My job required me to travel during most of the week. I was glad to be out of the house because it killed me to watch him self-destruct, but when I was gone, all I did was worry. I never knew anymore what I would wake up to or come home to. If I was on the road and he didn't answer the phone, I would imagine all sorts of horrible things.

He'd write me long letters telling me how much he loved me and how he couldn't bear how hard I had to work to keep us a float. At other times, he talked of suicide as being the only way he could take care of me. Everyone in his small hometown knew him, and he felt he had let all of them down. He never let people know how distraught he was or how severe his injuries really were.

It was at this point he knew he needed to get some help. He called the NFL Attorney Wayne Hooper and told him that he was having major psychological problems and had recurring thoughts of sui-cide.

The closest NFL doctor was in Oakland. Dr. Paul Berg had worked with some other NFL players. We didn't have the money to pay for the sessions, so Hooper told us that he would bill the NFL. Once Jeff had been deemed disabled from football and his "Line of Duty" started, ("Line of Duty" was temporary disability income of $870.00 that was issued for up to 60 months while filing for "Total and Permanent" Disability) they would reimburse us. For now, we would have to pay.

Jeff started seeing Dr. Berg weekly. He felt comfortable with him, and that was important if Jeff was going to move forward with his life. But the hour and a half drive took a toll on his neck, back, knees and ankle.

Before we knew it, the beautiful house we rented in Modesto was up for renewal and we couldn't afford the rent. I found a smaller house in a little subdivision a few miles away. It had a hot tub, which Jeff thought would help his neck and back.

Whenever his back pain was too much to bear, I would take him to the emergency room. His local doctor would admit him for a few days and put him on morphine drips. Sometimes during his stay, he would have panic attacks and break out in a cold sweat. On one occasion in the hospital he looked over at me, "I'm getting out of here, go get the car and meet me at the front door of the hospital."

"You're joking right?"

With an angry look he said, "No, I'm leaving now!"

"Honey, you don't have any clothes on and if you really want to leave, we need to check you out."

"I don't think you heard me, Brandi, I'm leaving with or without your help. So go get the car. They'll send us a bill and I don't give a damn about the clothes I came in with!"

He was serious; there was no arguing with him. I left his room and got the car. He pulled out his IV and came out of the hospital with nothing on but a hospital gown, still open in the back. He got in and I drove him home. You didn't argue with him when he got like that.

Dr. Berg suggested that Jeff write down his feelings and start a journal. At first, he resisted the idea, but once he started he couldn't stop. I decided to do the same. We would write to each other and it was very therapeutic for both of us. I don't think either one of us realized how much anger and hurt we both had inside.

Neither that realization nor the journaling stopped the drugs and there were still more days of him not wanting to live. I worried constantly. I knew I couldn't do this by myself anymore. I also started to realize just how much I had gotten away from my faith and how much, like Jeff, I was starting to lose hope. After praying about it, I knew I had to make some changes.

In the mid '70s my Mother turned me onto Dr. Robert Schuller, minister of the Crystal Cathedral in Garden Grove California.. His television show was called The Hour of Power. He became my minister when I lived in Southern California. I loved him because he didn't preach like a traditional preacher. He talked the way my father and grandfather talked to me and I was inspired by his messages.

I found him one day on a local Sacramento television station and rekindled my relationship with the church. I always had trouble turning everything over to God. I figured He didn't understand a lot of what I was going through, so I decided this time I would give him sixty percent of my problems and handle the other forty percent myself. God certainly wouldn't understand the forty percent that I had to hang on to.

As I started to regain my faith, I became more in tune to Jeff's spirituality, yet he never attended church. His parents would drop him off at church with his grandmother, but they didn't attend church and appear to be very religious. He had no interest either. He would say, "You have your God and I have mine."

Chapter 6

NFL Disability/Arbitration

By the end of 1982, we were turned down for Social Security Disability so I decided to appeal their decision and we were put on the docket for the next Social Security Circuit Judge. They would notify us when he would be in Modesto and I could plea our case–which I learned could take up to 18 months.

In the meantime, we decided to move to Turlock and rent a house from close friends of Jeff's parents. Soon after the move, we received a letter and apology from the NFL saying that they finally had a neutral physician in our area.

Jeff was sent to see Dr. Donald Trauner. Finally, someone who could confirm that he was disabled. The first devastating blow came in the form of a letter from the NFL Disability Benefits saying that Jeff had been denied benefits. Although he qualified for disability with over 80% back and neck injuries, Dr. Trauner said he could do "sedentary" work.

We asked, what the heck was "sedentary" work? They said it meant he could work a few hours per week in a job where he didn't have to move around. Whoa that would bring in the "Big Bucks".

This news was more than Jeff could handle and his hurt turned to anger. Trying to console him, I walked over and gave him a hug, "I'll help you honey. We'll just apply again and request to see another NFL doctor; we have to keep the faith and not lose hope."

He pushed me away, "Do what you want Brandi, it's a lost cause!"

Lost cause or not, I knew he deserved his pension and I wasn't going to give up. It wasn't just his future I was fighting for, but mine too. Every six months, I wrote letters of appeal to the NFL Board and Jeff would see another NFL appointed neutral physician. Every six months we were denied, stating that Jeff could still do "sedentary" work. It would reconfirm in Jeff's mind that it was a lost cause and reconfirm in my mind that we weren't going away that easily, and the NFL would remember who we were–because we wouldn't give up.

At one point we tried to go and see another doctor, but since the NFL neutral physicians are hired and paid by the NFL, we were not allowed to use any of our local physicians. I started doing research and found out at that time, there were only seven players who had ever been given NFL Football Disability income. The fight was on.

The NFL Board consisted of three players and three owners. At the NFL Board meeting in October 1983, they still couldn't come to any agreement about Jeff's disability. In one of the board meeting minutes that I acquired, one of the owners said, "What was Jeff's real reason for leaving football?"

It wasn't rocket science. His injuries were the reason. They finally agreed to send him to arbitration; it was risky, because if we lost, we could not appeal anymore. We knew Jeff was disabled. He had degenerative disc disease in his upper and lower back and neck. He had multiple injuries to his ankles and knee. He suffered severe headaches, psychological problems, and was addicted to prescription pain medication. We just wanted justice and to be able to get on with our lives.

They assigned us to an NFL arbitration attorney, former NFL Player, Alan Page. Alan worked for a large law firm in Minnesota, Lindquist and Venom. He would work with our local NFL appointed attorney, Wayne Hooper. We had no idea how long it would take to get to arbitration. Jeff had already been through months of psychological and NFL neutral physician examinations.

He stopped going to see Dr. Berg in Oakland because we had no money to pay his bill, which was now over $10,000. Jeff had insisted that we make monthly payments to him until he won his disability.

At this point, I knew I needed some professional help and guidance. I found a local psychiatrist in Turlock and started seeing him on a regular basis. He brought a lot of things to light about my own past. He felt that I was still having trouble dealing with my father's death. He told me that since I couldn't save my grandfather or my father from dying, I became a rescuer of people. This was an eye opener for me, because I could see he was right–especially regarding my marriage. He suggested that I confront Jeff again about getting some help too.

Jeff knew what all of this was doing to me. He even called several in and some local out-patient facilities. But as I stood there watching his body language, I knew he was just going through the motions. He realized that I saw through him, "I don't want to lose you, Brandi, but I don't think I can go someplace and be confined. If I'm going to do this, I have to do it my way."

"Don't do this for me honey, do it for you. I know I've given you an ultimatum, but in the end if you don't want to get help, it won't work. You know that, don't you?"

"I know I don't want to live like this the rest of my life. I'm so lost..." His bottom lip started to quiver.

"I know." Tears ran down my face. "You let me know what you decide. I've been seeing Dr. Smith here. I really like him. Maybe he could help you too."

I started to think about all of my own screw-ups in life, my own belief system about God and how my faith had been challenged most of my life. How could I fault Jeff? Who was I to make challenges for him? The Bible says "Lest we judge not." I saw that little boy lost. I remember when I was that little girl lost. A few days later, Jeff called while I was in Bakersfield working.

"B, I've been cold Turkey for the last few days and had a lot of time to think about what you said. Give me the phone number of your shrink and I'll make an appointment. If you're with me, I think I can kick this thing."

"I'm not going anywhere honey. I love you and I'm so proud of you."

For the first time in a long time our marriage was back on track. Therapy was working and our relationship was the best it had ever been. Jeff was like a different person, so we decided to try and have a baby. It gave him something to work towards. He still smoked pot, but had completely gone off his prescription drugs.

I thought a lot of his memory problems had been related to the amount of prescription drugs he was on, but I was starting to realize it was deeper than that. I wondered if something else could be contributing to his mood swings–but concussions had never crossed my mind, and they were not listed anywhere as a recognized NFL disability.

In May 1984, we got word that our NFL arbitration was set for July 26 and would take place in San Francisco. We felt things were starting to turn around. Then God tested my faith once again. While working in my office in Sacramento, I ran upstairs to answer the phone and tripped over my office manager's duffle bag. I wrenched my back and fell forward in an awkward position. I tried to catch myself before I hit the wall, but I missed and hit the floor hard.

I knew immediately that I had injured my lower back, part of me was working and the other half was not. I was slow to get up, tried work it off by walking around the office. Nothing helped. Embarrassed, I decided to head back to Modesto. The pain was excruciating as I made it down the stairs with the help of my office manager, and slowly got into my car.

It was an hour and a half back to Modesto. I realized after getting into the car, that I couldn't drive. I tried to get out of the car and go back upstairs, but I couldn't. I felt trapped and I started to panic. I looked around in the parking lot for someone to help me. It was such a helpless feeling.

I had no choice but to go for it and try to get back to Modesto. I started praying for God to help me and a few minutes after I got on the highway, I found a position where I put my foot up on the left side of the dash. A peace I can't explain came over me. I knew God was taking me home.

After pulling into the office parking lot, I slowly got out of the car and tried to walk, but couldn't. I knelt down to my knees beside the car. Fortunately, someone saw me on the pavement through the office window and ran out to help.

Mike didn't know what happened, but he could see I was in a lot of pain. I asked him to call Jeff and an ambulance to take me to the hospital.

The CAT scan showed that I had herniated two discs; L-5 and S-4. Because I had other neck and back problems, I was not a good candidate for surgery, so my neurologist sent me home with complete bed rest. He showed Jeff how to place me in the bed. After six weeks, I was able to go to physical therapy, which would continue until I could return to work.

I was scared. With Jeff not able to work, I couldn't afford to be ill or sick. I pleaded with my boss and they allowed me to work by phone from home, provided my offices stayed profitable. Once I explained my situation to my clients, they came together to help me, my offices did better than ever and I managed to keep my job. Jeff was so loving and attentive. It was nice to be taken care of for a change.

While I was recuperating, we got a letter from Social Security that our court date was set for July 12 at the courthouse in downtown Modesto. The time at home would help me to prepare for the case.

We were also preparing for Jeff's arbitration case. Alan Page really knew his stuff, plus he'd been a player. He was so refreshing. Through him, we found that Hooper failed to file for Jeff's total and permanent disability. He had only filed for Jeff's temporary Line of Duty, which was only $870 per month. Alan immediately filed for total and permanent disability.

Jeff contacted Gene Upshaw, who was now head of the players' union, to come in as a character witness. Gene agreed and sent a letter to Jeff, reiterating about Jeff's love for the game and how he always gave over 100% for the team.

July 12 was here before we knew it. I represented Jeff in the SSI case. I was still recuperating, but I was determined to do it and knew the case better than anyone else. I went in holding my head up high. It was standing room only. I was thankful I was number two on the docket. I presented fifty-six exhibits which included all of Jeff's physical and emotional disabilities. Although the SSI Judge seemed to be impressed, we would have to wait for his decision after he reviewed everything.

Our NFL arbitration was next. Alan Page flew in a few days early to meet with Jeff and Wayne Hooper. He told Jeff that our NFL arbitrator was Sam Kagel.

The morning of the arbitration, there was a big surprise. Gene Upshaw was a no-show. He was going to be a very important witness for Jeff. By him not showing up, we knew where his loyalty was–it wasn't with Jeff. Because he had taken on the position as head of the NFL Players Union, it was obvious that he didn't want to rock that boat. Jeff was very hurt and disappointed.

The NFL walked into the arbitration room with six attorneys. The odds were against Jeff from the start; however, Alan Page knew what he was doing. He was brilliant!

Sam Kagel made his decision that Jeff Winans was totally disabled from football and was to be granted total and permanent football disability income as long as he remained disabled and unable to work. His disability pension would be retroactive for six months.

Having hope when there wasn't any, and staying persistent, paid off. Three years of hell was over–or so we thought.

Chapter 7

The Gunshot Accident

With Jeff's disability income starting, September 6, 1984, we decided to make an offer on the house we had been renting in Turlock, and the sellers accepted.

A month before we were to close, the deal fell through. One of their sons decided to move back from Spain with his new wife. Knowing the family (Jeff had known them his whole life) we backed out with no hard feelings. But with both of us injured, the timing couldn't have been worse.

We were lucky to find a house only a few miles away. It was a large two-story, Spanish-style home with a large family room and a large, fenced-in backyard. We liked that because I was trying to get pregnant.

On the morning of November 13, 1984, as I left for work, Jeff stood waiting on his friend Greg, to help move the last of our things out. There were mixed emotions, as we really had wanted to buy this house, but we knew there was a new beginning waiting for us at the new house.

Around noon, I left work in Modesto and headed over to the new house. I was still recovering from my back injury so I was only working half days. When I arrived, the garage door was up, but no one was there. I assumed they were on their way with another load.

After waiting a few minutes, I remembered that I still had things to get out of the refrigerator and decided to drive over to the other house to see if I could help. As I turned down our street, I saw a police car in front of our house and my father-in-law's station wagon in the driveway. It didn't seem out of the ordinary because one of our collector cars had recently been vandalized and Jeff had been using his Dad's station wagon to move.

When I pulled into the driveway, the garage door remote wouldn't work, so I opened my car door, got out and walked toward the garage to see what was wrong. Just then, a policeman and my father-in-law came out the front door. The policeman in the car got out and headed toward me. I could see that my father-in-law was very upset and my gut told me something bad had happened.

The officers walked toward me, "Mrs. Winans? Your husband has had an accident."

"What kind of accident"?

"Jeff accidentally shot himself with a handgun and he's on his way to the hospital."

"Oh my God! What happened? Where did he shoot himself?

I looked over at my father-in-law. Tears were starting to roll down his face. He was too upset to speak. There appeared to be more to the story, by the look on their faces.

"It appeared to be his right leg."

"Just a wound to the leg," I asked with relief.

"Yes Ma'am and you need to stay out of the house until the investigators arrive and finish their investigation."

"Where did they take him?

"To Emanuel," Glenn said getting his composure back. "Go on over and I'll be there in a few minutes."

My emotions were all over the place. I gave my father-in-law a hug and headed to the hospital.

I arrived a few minutes later. I knew I had to keep it together as I walked up to the admissions desk.

"Hi, I'm Brandi Winans. My husband, Jeff, was brought in by ambulance a few minutes ago with a gunshot wound to his leg. Can you direct me to where he is, please?"

The nurse seemed to just ignore me. When I asked her again

I thought she went to see where he was, but she never came back. With my patience now very thin, I walked over to another nurse who looked like she was in charge. She looked up at me and our eyes met.

In a calm tone of voice I said, "My husband, Jeff Winans, has come in with a gunshot wound to his leg. I have been patiently waiting for almost fifteen minutes. If you can't help me, I will search every ER bed until I find him, and if necessary I will make a spectacle of myself," adding a half-smile at the end.

The nurse saw I was serious. She turned around and motioned for me to follow. We walked a few steps and she pointed at a curtain. "Thank you," I said.

I took deep breath as the nurse turned and walked away, and then I slowly let it out as I pulled the curtain back. "Oh God," I gasped. Jeff was lying on the bed. I could see that he was in so much pain from the look on his face. He was grasping onto the bed sheet with a clinched fist. I looked down at his leg and saw blood coming out of a large hole just below his right knee.

Then he started screaming, "Get the 'F' out of here!!"

I thought he must be talking to someone behind me so I turned around, but no one was there.

I walked toward him and he said in a louder tone "Brandi, didn't you hear me? I said "Get the 'F' out of here!"

I was so confused. Why was he talking to me like that? What did I do?

A moment later, a different nurse came in. "Mrs. Winans you'll have to wait in the waiting room. Please, Mrs. Winans." Her eyes motioned for me to leave, as she took my hand and walked me back to the ER waiting room.

I sat down, my heart pounding. Tears started rolling down my face as I stared at a cold white wall. What was going on? I'm his wife. Why was he so cruel? Did he mean what he said?

Within a few minutes, my father-in-law, Glenn, arrived and told me what he thought had happened from the evidence and the 911 call. Apparently, Jeff was waiting for Greg to come and help with the last load. He went into the bedroom and took some folded jeans out of the top part of the closet, then grabbed some other things off the bed. From there he walked down the hall and into the kitchen. The COP.357 derringer I had bought him a few months before fell out of the clothes.

I had no idea that a few months before, he borrowed two .357 magnum shells from his friend Paul. After he loaded the derringer, instead of putting it back in the case where it belonged, he put it in between a pair of jeans and forgot about it until the day of the move. I never understood why he had not put the gun back in the case.

When the gun hit the floor, it went off, hitting him just below the right knee. Jeff dropped to the floor. He had no idea what happened. Then he saw the derringer lying on the kitchen floor and remembered he had put it in the jeans in the closet.

In excruciating pain, he dragged himself over to the phone and called 911. Blood was gushing out of his leg like a garden hose. He knew from being an Eagle Scout that unless he could stop the bleeding, he would bleed to death within a few minutes.

He grabbed the clothes he had been carrying and made a tourniquet on his upper right thigh. Then he remembered that the front door was locked, so he dragged himself over, unlocked it, and dragged himself back into the kitchen where he waited for the ambulance.

Before calling 911, he called Greg and asked him to come over and clean up this mess before I got home. Greg never made it.

From the 911 call, the police called Jeff's father. The Winans family has a lot of history in Turlock. Jeff's grandfather was a fallen policeman who was in killed in action in 1948 and Jeff was one of the local town football heroes.

I asked Glenn where Janice, Jeff's Mom, was, when he came to the hospital. He made no comment. A nurse came over and called me to admissions so I could fill out the paperwork.

As I was going back to the waiting room an ER Doctor came over.

"I'm sorry, Mrs. Winans, but it's not looking good. Jeff has lost a lot of blood so we have to do some blood transfusions. We are taking him for an arteriogram to assess the damage to the leg, and are trying to get hold of Dr. John Andrews. He's an excellent vascular surgeon here in town."

"I don't care about the leg," I pleaded, "just please save my husband!"

As I was speaking to the doctor, I saw Jeff out of the corner of my eye being wheeled on his way to the arteriogram.

When he saw me, he blurted out, "Brandi, Brandi, I'm sorry. Please let them know my tolerance to pain medication and make sure they give me a lot! Please! I'm in so much pain! Please!"

His voice was cracking and tears were running down his face.

"All right, I'll make sure. It's going to be all right. I love you."

"I love you too," he wailed.

In a sick way, I had to find some humor in him wanting me to make sure that he would be given enough drugs for his pain. They had no idea how much his tolerance had been before he went off all the pain medication he had been on.

Glenn and I walked back to the waiting room and sat down. They said the arteriogram would take about an hour, but it seemed to take forever. We were going into two hours when I asked one of the ER nurses if she could check on Jeff. She came back and said it wouldn't be much longer.

Finally, the radiologist opened the door.

"May we speak outside, please?" I grabbed Glenn's hand and we walked out together.

"Jeff has lost a lot of blood. The arteriogram showed that there is nothing alive from about his mid-thigh down. We are preparing him for surgery and we are waiting for Dr. Andrews to get here. He will be performing the surgery on Jeff."

"Is he good at what he does?"

"Yes, Mrs. Winans. Dr. Andrews helped write the micro-vascular books with world renowned, Dr. Harry Buncke. They were in Vietnam together. We are getting as much blood as we have in stock right now. He will need more transfusions later if he makes it through tonight. There is a new epidemic called AIDS."

"What is AIDS?"

"It stands for Auto Immune Deficiency Syndrome."

I thought, gee, Doc, that told me a lot. "I don't understand."

"One of the ways the disease is transmitted is through blood transfusions. If he does make it through today, he'll need more blood. I suggest you get family members and friends to donate, so you know where it came from. You can call Irwin Blood Bank,they will help you."

"Irwin Blood Bank?"

"Out of San Francisco. They can bring a blood donor truck in and you can request that all of the blood donated goes to Jeff. But first, we have to get him through today. I'm sorry I don't have better news. Quite frankly, I don't know how he's still alive. The fact that he stayed conscious and made a tourniquet on his leg is a miracle. The average Joe would have bled to death."

We thanked the doctor and Glenn called Janice. It had been almost three hours. I needed to call my mother and brother in Florida and tell them what was going on before they found about it on the news. As I dialed the phone, the day was starting to catch up with me. I was nauseous. My voice was cracking as she answered the phone.

"Hi, Mom," I said trying to contain myself. "There's been an accident." I took a deep breath. Tears began flowing. "Jeff accidentally shot himself. It doesn't look good. He may not make it out of surgery." I paused, taking another deep breath. Tears were continuing to flow, "Will you put him on the prayer line?"

She started crying. "Oh my God, Brandi, of course I will. Call me when he's out of surgery. I don't care what time it is!"

"Okay", was all I could muster.

"Will you promise me?"

"Yes Mom, I promise."

"Where is Janice?

"I don't know. She hasn't been here yet."

"What"? This is her only son!"

"I don't know, Mom. Glenn is calling her now and giving her an update. Thank God he's been here with me. "

I started to cry again. "Tell Steve to call me when he can. For now, Mom, please, just pray… I love you".

"I love you, too. I wish I could be there with you."

"I wish you could, too, but I understand."

My mother had recently fallen going into her apartment and fractured several vertebrae in her back. She had been laid up for three weeks and had a very long recovery ahead of her. I could relate from my own back injuries.

My brother Steve was on location for CBS, so neither one of them would be able to come to California.

The afternoon passed and Jeff was still in surgery. The day was taking a toll on my back. I asked the nurse for a pad so I could lie down on the floor, elevate my legs and take the pressure off my lower spine. To my surprise, she wheeled in a chair similar to our Lazy Boy.

Around seven, I couldn't stand it anymore. Someone had to tell me what was going on. I walked over to the nurse's station "My husband has been in surgery for over five hours. Can you please check on him for me?"

She looked up and said, "He's still in surgery, Mrs. Winans. When we know more, we will tell you. I know it's hard, but try to be patient."

Glenn got us some coffee. There was nothing on the news about it.

Thank God it hadn't hit the media yet. I had to get out of the waiting room, so I let the nurse know we were going for a walk down the hall.

My mind was racing, I kept thinking of the last time I saw Jeff, when they wheeled him down the hall for the arteriogram. It might be the last time I will see him alive. I had to get those kinds of thoughts out of my head, stay positive and keep my faith in God to take care of him.

Around half past eight, my mother-in-law, Janice, showed up. I gave her a hug. I could feel the tension and asked her if she had called Jeff's sisters. She didn't respond. She was talking a million miles a minute. Then she started pacing. I could see she was very distraught.

"Janice, would you like to take a walk with me?"

She grabbed my arm, "Yes Brandi, let's take a walk."

As we walked down the hall her hand was squeezing my arm tighter and tighter. She just kept saying, "It's going to be all right, everything is going to be all right."

We got back to the waiting room and a nurse said the surgery was over and they would be taking Jeff to recovery and then to ICU. "Doctor Andrew will be out in a few minutes to update you on your husband's condition."

"Thank you."

I looked at my watch. It was a quarter to ten. A few minutes later they wheeled an unconscious Jeff out of OR, Janice looked at him and started screaming, "JEFF! JEFF!" and fell to the floor. Glenn and I rushed over and helped her back up. She was hysterical, sobbing uncontrollably.

I realized why she hadn't been to the hospital. It was too much for her. It was always very hard for her to show emotion, and she didn't realize was how much her son needed her. Dr. Andrew finally came out to see us. There was no smile on his face. I knew that the news was not going to be good.

"Mrs. Winans, I'm Dr. Andrew. Jeff is still in critical condition, but we have him stable for now. We have repaired all we can today. If he makes it through the night, we will go back in tomorrow afternoon and do some more repairs. He's lost a lot of blood and his other bodily functions are starting to shut down. For now, what is left of the leg is still there. I am going to consult with my friend, Dr. Harry Buncke in San Francisco tonight. All we can do now is wait and pray."

I thanked him for his honesty, and then looked over to my in-laws who were exhausted. The rescuer in me took over. "Why don't you guys go home and get some rest? I'll call you if there's any change."

Janice was in no condition to stay and Glenn agreed to go home for now. The orderly pushed the Lazy Boy chair into Jeff's ICU room. Janice was upset that I was staying. I didn't care, I wasn't leaving. I couldn't sleep anyway. I watched the monitors and listened to the sound of his heartbeat. He had a needle or tube everywhere. His right leg was heavily bandaged and elevated above his heart with what looked like a sling. But I had never seen him look so peaceful.

Our whole life together, the good, the bad and the ugly, was running through my head. It's funny how when that happens, only the good seems to remain. I loved him so much. My emotions were so deep; I never took my eyes off him. I think I was still in shock.

Before I knew it, I saw the reflection of the sun coming up through the blinds. I looked at my watch. It was six am. Jeff was still alive. A peace came over me as my eyes slowly closed. I slept for a couple of hours until I heard the doctor come in.

"Jeff, good morning. Mr. Winans, wake up. Can you open your eyes for me?"

I opened my eyes and saw the doctor and nurse standing along his bedside closest to the door. I looked over at Jeff. His eyes were still closed. I sat up and started calling his name. "Jeff, honey, wake up. Jeff, wake up, honey."

I touched his arm and caressed it. Slowly, he opened his eyes. He was very groggy and turned his head toward me trying to move. His agony reflected on his face. Dr. Andrew ordered more pain medication for him and decided to push the next surgery up to early afternoon. I called Glenn and Janice to let them know. Glenn said he would be over around noon. By the time I came back to ICU, Jeff was out again.

I was starting to get nauseous again. It hit me that I hadn't eaten anything since yesterday. Maybe some crackers would help. I told the nurse I was going to get something to eat and if anything happened to come and get me. She assured me that she would.

As I walked by the pay phones, I realized that I had forgotten to call Mom. She was worried sick. She had Jeff on the prayer line and I was sure that she called everyone she knew to get them to pray for him. She was doing all of this with a broken back. I had two herniated discs and Jeff had almost shot his leg off and could be on his deathbed. What a family. I updated Mom on Jeff's next surgery. She had not been able to reach my brother Steve. My emotions were tumbling over themselves and I forgot to tell her what hospital we were in.

I felt a little better after I ate some crackers. I was grungy, so I went to the bathroom and took a sponge bath with some paper towels from the wall dispenser. The water on my face and arms felt so good. It would be nice to have a shower and a change of clothes. Rinsing my mouth out with mouthwash, I headed back to ICU.

When I walked in, Jeff was awake, but very weak. This time he was glad to see me. I walked over and gave him a kiss, holding his hand so tight, caressing his fingers. He was still in so much pain.

The nurse came, "Jeff got a few phone calls while you were gone."

"Did they leave any messages?"

She gave me the look that said, "I'm not your personal answering machine." She did have a point. We smiled at each other.

"Can you see about getting him some more pain medication?"

Jeff dozed off after the injection. I started to wonder if he would survive this next surgery. He had lost so much blood. I found the hospital chapel and got on my knees and prayed. I usually could keep it together in a crisis, but this time I was falling apart. Maybe it was because I only had two hours of sleep and this had been very emotional twenty-four hours. Maybe it was something else.

Chapter 8

The Blessing

With everything I was going through, I needed a distraction and started thinking about how nice it would be to have a change of clothes and a hot bath. I just needed to get out of the hospital for a little while.

I decided to drive over to the house on El Camino. I still had stuff in the refrigerator that needed to be cleaned out. As I pulled into the driveway, I could see the yellow tape from the police was still there. An eerie feeling came over me as I pulled the tape off the front door, unlocked it and walked in.

It looked like a war zone. It smelled like death. There was blood on the floor and all over the kitchen and foyer walls. Some of the blood was so thick, it appeared to be fresh. The main puddle of blood was where Jeff had spent the most time waiting for the ambulance. I could see streaks of blood where he drug himself over to open the front door. The phone, smeared with blood, lay on the floor.

It was too much emotion to deal with. I ran out the front door, got in my car, put my head on the steering wheel, closed my eyes and just sat there. I couldn't get the vision out of my mind; where Jeff had laid on the floor, all the blood on the kitchen wall. I started the car, screeched out of the driveway and went back to the hospital.

When I arrived back at ICU, Jeff was waiting to go back into surgery. His voice was very hoarse from the tubes they had stuck down his throat and nose the day before.

His doctor said they had to create a new artery by placing a catheter in Jeff's spine to the part of the artery that was left, then take another vein and graph it to the artery. The catheter was to enlarge the vein and, hopefully, produce enough blood flow as it graphed onto the other vein. It was the only chance to keep any part of the leg.

They came for Jeff around one o'clock. Tears ran down the sides of his face. I tried to be strong when they wheeled him out, and gave him a reassuring smile. In the back of my mind I thought about the last time I saw my Dad alive. Would life replay itself? Would this be the last time I would see Jeff alive?

His father arrived as they were taking him down the hall to the operating room. We both knew how serious this surgery was and I grabbed Glenn's hand as he watched his only son being wheeled down the corridor.

Four hours later, the doctor came out. They wouldn't know if the surgery was successful right away. If it was, they may be able to save the leg. If it wasn't, they would have to amputate. He was alive, but in critical condition–with a new complication. The antibiotics they were giving him weren't working. We didn't know how much if any damage was done to his liver, or kidneys or heart from all the blood he had lost. It was still touch and go.

The AP Wire and the local newspapers had picked the story up and put out the word that Jeff needed blood. One of his former coaches at Modesto Junior College called to say that he was going to have the members of the football team donate blood.

I called Irwin Blood Bank in San Francisco and they drove down to Modesto and set up their truck. I didn't understand this thing they were calling AIDS and I didn't have time to think about anything right now except Jeff.

When I was told what the Modesto Junior College team was doing, I remembered that the following evening was the 49ers' Pop Warner banquet. Since I hadn't been home, I needed to find out if the autographed San Francisco 49ers' football had come in the mail. Jeff founded the first Pop Warner Football Team in Turlock earlier that year. Since we were so close to San Francisco, he called them the Turlock 49er's. They were excited that he called them the 49ers' and said they would have the team sign one and send it out in time for our first banquet.

The families of the kids on the team had been selling tickets to raffle off the football at the banquet. I didn't have their number. I had to remember to call later.

I called my office to let them know what had happened. Mike said not to worry, he heard about it on the radio that morning on his way to work, he had been trying to reach me and already called corporate to let them know about Jeff's accident. They told me to take as much time off as I needed.

Minutes turned into hours and hours turned into another day. I was stubborn and wouldn't go home. What home? Jeff and I were finally working things out. It had been the best year of our marriage. Now he may never come home, and I was determined that he would not be alone if God decided to take him.

Glenn stopped in on his way home and invited me to dinner. My sister-in-law Shari had come down from Sunnyvale and said she would stay with Jeff until I got back. I was feeling sick to my stomach again and went in to the bathroom and threw up. I looked like death warmed over, but Shari convinced me to go to dinner.

"Brandi, I'll call you at Mom's or you can call me here every thirty minutes."

"All right," I uttered, "All right."

The autographed football for the Pop Warner banquet arrived late that afternoon. I knew the football was important to Jeff because it was for the kids. I dropped it off on the way to dinner, and started crying again.

It was pouring down rain and I could hardly see, but I got to my in-laws, pulled in their driveway, then sat in the car trying to fix my face. I went in the side kitchen door from the patio. Janice was cooking dinner. She took one look and started to lecture me.

"Brandi, you are spending way too much time at the hospital. You need to go home so Jeff can get his rest."

I didn't need to hear this from her. She had been to the hospital only once since the accident. By this time I was in a very fragile state of mind. "Janice, he may be your son, but he's my husband and I'll stay at the hospital until he's out of danger. In fact, I think I am going home, take a hot shower and go back to the hospital–because if I stay here, I'm going to say something that I will regret."

I turned around, walked out the door, got into my car and drove to our new house. It was still pouring down rain and my emotions were running wild.

My family doctor had prescribed some Valium for me that I had filled at the hospital pharmacy the day after the accident. After my mother-in-law incident, I was ready for one. When I opened the door from the garage into the house, I took the bottle out of my purse and tried to open it up. The childproof top opened up too quick and the pills went everywhere. I bent over and scooped up as many as I could. For a moment, I knew what it must feel like to be a drug addict. As I went to put a Valium in my mouth, a little voice said, "Are you sure you want to take that?"

"Ah, yes I'm sure."

Then the little voice asked, "What if you're pregnant?"

Pregnant? Pregnant was the farthest thing on my mind. I had been sick the last few days and I was throwing up, but I assumed it was because I was upset over the gunshot accident. I remembered there was a leftover pregnancy test I unpacked a few days before in the upstairs bathroom. As I headed towards the stairs, I started thinking about the first time we had made love since my herniated discs. We hadn't used any protection because I had been trying to get pregnant.

Impatient, the pregnancy test seemed to take forever, but in the end it was positive. It hit me like a ton of bricks. I called Dr. Moen, my OBGYN at home and asked him if I could have a blood test. He arranged for me to have it the next morning.

Could this be the miracle we needed? Was the turning point of a bad season finally over, or was God going to take Jeff and leave me with a baby?

I got undressed, turned on the shower and got in. The warm water was heaven as it ran down my back. I thought about people in third world countries and our soldiers overseas who go days, sometimes weeks, months without being able to bathe. I felt so renewed and blessed.

I wouldn't know for sure if I was pregnant until tomorrow, so I decided not to say anything when I got back to the hospital. Jeff was sleeping and for the first time in days, I felt some peace. The blood work was done the next morning at nine and two hours later it was confirmed. I was about six weeks pregnant.

Dr. Andrews was there when I walked into Jeff's ICU room. He looked up as I was smiling from ear to ear. Then I blurted it out, "I just got my blood work back this morning. We're going to have a baby!"

Everyone started to smile as the doctor and nurses congratulated me. Jeff was sleeping peacefully but I couldn't wait another minute to tell him. I started rubbing his arm and playing with his fingers, then whispered in his ear, "Honey, I'm pregnant and you're going to be fine because this child's going to need a father." I kept repeating it over and over again very softly.

Slowly he opened his eyes. "Honey, I had some blood work done this morning, we're going to have a baby."

He looked at me, very childlike, "We are? A baby?"

"Yes honey, we're going to have a baby."

He closed his eyes and smiled.

Glenn and Shari were sitting in the waiting room so I decided to let them know the good news. They could see how excited I was and were a little puzzled.

"I have some great news. I just found out I'm pregnant. We're gonna have a baby. I told Jeff, but I'm not sure if he'll remember." They were shocked but seemed to be very happy about the news.

By the time I saw Janice again, Glenn had told her the good news. She was very happy about the baby. This would be their first grandchild. I knew in my heart that telling Jeff about the baby would give him a reason to live, where so many times before he had wanted to die.

The football team had donated enough blood and then some for Jeff's blood bank.

We decided to let Jeff name the baby in case something did happen to him. He decided that if it was a boy, we would name him Travis and if it was a girl, we would name her Amanda.

As the news started to travel from the AP Wire, we got bombarded with phone calls, letters and get well cards from people all over the United States. It was very moving and very emotional. It meant so much to us, especially to Jeff, and he realized how when there's a crisis, people come together

While I was at my OBGYN, Jeff got a call from Al Davis, the owner of the Oakland Raiders. Al told Jeff that he was sorry to hear about the accident. Knowing that Jeff was still in critical condition, he told him he knew how much the Super Bowl ring meant to him. He said if Jeff would drop the 12 Million Dollar lawsuit against him and the Raiders, he would get him his ring.

To my surprise, Jeff agreed. It was at that moment I realized how much that ring and playing football meant to him. Maybe this would put all the anger, resentment and bitterness behind us.

Within a few weeks, Jeff's surgeries had started to wind down. He was out of ICU for now, but infection was Jeff's greatest enemy and it kept coming back in different forms. Because of the gunshot, his leg was cut open from where the bullet entered just below his knee, all the way down to his ankle. The bone was hollow where the bullet originally entered so I nicknamed the wound the "Black Hole."

Every few days, a new roll of gauze was stuffed down the hole. Then it would have to be removed and changed. Once the bone is exposed, infections become prominent. As soon as they got one infection under control, another one requiring a different antibiotic would pop up, so Jeff was sent for special testing every three weeks. We started calling the drugs elephant antibiotics. The possible side effects from them were not pretty. He could go blind, lose his hearing, suffer kidney failure or all of the above.

My back improved to the point that I was finally able to go back to work full-time. As I made the rounds at one of the claims offices in Modesto, my friend Bill Trubitsky said in a very concerned voice, "I'm so sorry to hear about Jeff. Have you contacted a lawyer?"

"Why? It was an accident." I never thought of any repercussion, much less a lawsuit. Jeff was alive and I was pregnant. I had more important things on my mind.

"It wouldn't hurt. What if the gun was defective?" He said if the gun was defective, we might be able to sue the sporting goods store that sold it to me, or the gun manufacturer. "I'll have my friend George call you for an appointment /consultation."

"Thanks Bill."

I saw George Anderson the next week. He was amazed at my story. He had read the articles in the paper, but didn't know all the details. He was very moved that Jeff's junior college football team had come together and donated blood. He asked me to bring the gun into his office so he could have it tested for any defects. I dropped the gun off at his office the following week. Meanwhile I had to concentrate on my family.

Chapter 9

It's a Boy

Over the next few months, Jeff was subjected to multiple surgeries. The good news was the antibiotics they had him on were finally working. I was four months pregnant and had already gained twenty-five pounds. We began to wonder if we were having more than one, but according to the sonograms and Dr. Moen this was not the case.

He sent me for an amniocentesis in Fresno, which the state of California requires for anyone pregnant who is over thirty-four. My mother-in-law was able to drive me and I felt it helped us to bond a little. The procedure was very uncomfortable. They placed a large needle in my abdomen and took out embryonic fluids. I thought at one moment I was going to miscarry after the procedure, due to the heavy cramping, but it subsided after forty minutes.

Three weeks after the procedure, I got the call from the hospital. I was a nervous wreck. I could not take any more traumas right now. This baby had given both of us so much to live for now.

"Mrs. Winans, this is Nurse Jenny. We have the results of your tests and I need to go over everything with you." I took a deep breath.

"Everything is normal."

"Everything's Okay?"

"Yes, would you and your husband like to know the sex of your baby?" We were praying for a boy, but we wouldn't turn down a girl. The baby's health was the most important thing.

"Oh yes."

"It's a boy. Congratulations".

I was so overwhelmed with joy. "Thank you, thank you so much."

I couldn't wait to get to the hospital to tell Jeff. I walked into his room smiling from ear to ear, and gave him a very wet kiss. Buy now he looked like a caveman. He was skin and bones. His dark curly hair was long, and he had grown a beard to cover up his hollowed out cheeks. He certainly wasn't prepared for a kiss like that.

"Guess what? The hospital called and we got the results back from the amnio. The baby is fine. It's a boy!"

Jeff put his hand on my stomach, "We're having a boy?" Tears rolled down the side of his face, "We're having a boy? He said with excitement. Hi son, Hi Travis."

It was a beautiful moment. "Travis it is," I said, leaned over and kissed him again. "I can't wait for you to come home. I miss you so much and I'm gonna make sure that you don't miss a thing."

Just then Travis kicked me. It was like he was listening and he approved. We just smiled and looked at each other. God does work in mysterious ways. Once again, things were looking up and hopefully Jeff would be home soon.

The next morning at my office in Modesto, I got a call from our corporate hospitalization department in Ohio. The supervisor said there was a problem with my insurance.

When I was hired, they gave me a two million dollar health policy for Jeff and myself. The monthly premiums were automatically taken out of my paycheck. The nationwide company I worked for was self–insured and they fell under the protection of something called "The Erisa Act." (Just like the NFL)

"What's the problem?" I asked jokingly.

"We have a problem continuing coverage for your husband."

"What do you mean?"

"I'm sorry, Mrs. Winans, but we have never had a situation like this before. After much discussion, we decided that unless your husband's leg is amputated, we will no longer be able to cover his injury. Any further medical expenses will be deemed medically unnecessary."

"I don't understand?" I was devastated. After everything we had been through–and now this. "How can you do that? Our plan says he's insured for up to two million dollars. I won't ask my husband to cut off his leg to keep our insurance. If he decides to amputate it will be his decision, not yours, not mine, but his! I'm going to seek some legal advice!"

"I'm sorry Mrs. Winans, do what you feel you need to," she replied.

I hung up the phone.

"Hey Brandi, you look like you just saw a ghost," Mike said joking around.

I told Mike about what the hospitalization department had just told me.

"What's next Mike? What's next? What else can they do to us? Take away my medical insurance too? Not pay for the baby?"

"What're you going to do," he asked.

"I'm going to talk to George Anderson and see what he has to say. I'm not going to say anything to Jeff until I find out if we have any recourse."

I put a call into George and headed to the hospital after work. The hospital food sucked and my daily routine was to stop by and pick food up or make dinner and take it to Jeff. Today, he was awake and in a good mood.

As I waddled into his hospital room, he commented on how big I was getting. He would find newspaper articles about women having big babies and cut them out. One time he cut out an article of a baby born weighing over sixteen pounds and wrote on it: "This Could Be Us." Not if I could help it.

While I was there, the doctor came in gave us the news we had been praying for–Jeff could go home on a trial basis. The last trial had not gone very well, and within forty-eight hours we were rushing him back in an ambulance. But he had come a long way since then.

I kept thinking about his insurance. What if something else happened? Would it be covered? How was I going to tell him that we might not have any more insurance? What was I going to do?

George's secretary called to tell me she was able to get me in to see him the next afternoon. He was familiar with the Erisa Act. It wasn't good. Large self-insured corporations used it as an umbrella.

I had faith in the man upstairs and I remembered someone saying, "If God takes you to it, He'll get you through it." As long as we kept the faith, I knew somehow he would. I made up my mind then that Big Brother was not going to ruin our lives anymore, but I needed this job more than ever. Jeff's small NFL pension couldn't pay the bills.

George came into the conference room. "Brandi, we have confirmation from our gun expert in Minnesota that the gun you bought Jeff was defective."

My emotions were overpowering me. "Well, if the gun was defective and Buffalo Arms (the gun manufacturer) is out of business, then that's it. There's no need to continue."

"It's true, the company that made the .357 Derringer is no longer in business. We did find out that the maker was a Tonawanda, New York Policeman, who basically manufactured guns out of his garage and sold them to the gun distributor. They in turn distributed them to gun and sporting good stores. There is no recourse with him. His liability insurance ended when he folded the company. There is the possibility of suing the sporting goods store where you purchased the gun in Modesto. They usually have liability insurance. I'll check it out and the gun distributor.

"Tell me more about why you needed to see me today."

I could feel my cheeks getting wet as I told him about the phone call from my company and what they had said regarding Jeff's insurance. He couldn't believe they wanted Jeff's leg amputated or they would not pay anymore bills.

"Don't worry. Let me see what I can find out. You worry about that baby you're carrying and your husband. Let me worry about the other stuff right now."

I had felt so alone the last few months. Maybe it was because I was pregnant and the combination of everything else. Some days were extremely overwhelming, but today I left feeling as if I wasn't alone. Someone else was fighting for us.

I knew I had to keep my faith. There were times when I looked up at the Lord and said, "You and I have to talk. You said you wouldn't give me more than I could handle. Hello? Is there anybody listening up there, cause I can't take anymore right now God. I can't take anymore!"

George called the corporate hospitalization department to find out what was going on. They told him what they had told me; they were deeming everything medically unnecessary until the leg was amputated. Once that happened, they would re-evaluate things. How can companies be allowed to do this to people? How can a guy sit in his garage and be allowed to make guns?

After doing some research I learned about the Federal Gun Laws of 1968. It required a gun to have minimal specifications: barrel, a trigger, handle, etc. You and I could sit in our garage and make a gun, get a distributor and no one would have any legal recourse if it didn't work or it was defective.

George also found out that the gun distributor did not test their weapons and that was the information we needed to go after them. The distributor was still in business and happened to be one of the largest distributors in the country.

So July 1985, we filed a lawsuit for $1.5 million dollars against the distributor. It turned out that the insurance on the sporting goods store where I bought the gun had lapsed three days before the accident.

Then more of the unexpected happened. Once my company confirmed the lawsuit we had against the distributor, they implemented what they called a third party subrogation clause allowing them to sue Jeff and me personally, and put a lien on the lawsuit we had against the distributor. Third party subrogation was not in my benefit book when Jeff had the accident, but adding it now gave them the right to go after us for the money they had already paid out.

That same month, after developing toxemia, I went out on early maternity leave and worked from home again until the baby was born. Jeff came home from another bout in the hospital and was finally able to go with me on one of my check-ups.

He had never seen a sonogram and grinned from ear to ear as he watched his son suck his thumb and kick my belly. Travis was a little wiggle worm in my womb. He moved constantly. It was as if he was saying, "Let me out, let me out." Believe me, I couldn't wait to let him out. I had gained sixty-eight pounds and had a fifty-two inch waist.

The creditor calls were now constant. Before I went on maternity leave, I was hoping they would just go away. They didn't. Very few understood. The hospital was okay for now, after talking to them–only because of Jeff's celebrity status. I knew it wouldn't be long before they would start making demands too. Jeff had recovered enough to where I thought he could handle it. If something happened to me in delivery, he would have to be abreast of everything.

After learning everything that had been going on, he suggested that we file for bankruptcy. I was too stubborn because if we did that it would mean they had won. Right then all I could think about was working and having this baby.

Friday morning, August 2, 1985, I got up at five-thirty to let our cat "Cat" out. I bent over to change his water dish and felt something warm run down my leg. I thought my bladder was leaking, then realized that my water had broken, I was going into labor.

I went upstairs and woke Jeff from a very groggy sleep. He had trouble sleeping and the doctor had given him sleeping pills called Halcyon. First he was grumpy, then very excited as he slowly got up and got dressed. I called the hospital and we were on our way to Modesto, about thirty minutes north of Turlock.

My labor was getting stronger when we arrived around seven. I was scheduled for a C-section on August 6 because of my toxemia. Dr. Moen, was heading out for a weekend outing with his family to Lake Tahoe. The hospital reached him just as he was leaving.

They started an IV right away and put me on Pitocin, which induces labor, while Jeff called our friend Luisa and his parents. The birthing room was very tiny and only had room for one small chair and Jeff. It was hard on him but he was determined to be there with me.

I, on the other hand, was hurting, moaning and turning into one nasty woman. This was something I learned later was typical for a pregnant woman in labor who at those moments hated all men.

He said, "Breathe, Honey."

I angrily replied, "I am breathing!"

We laughed about it later.

At two o'clock in the afternoon, after going for the natural birth, I couldn't stand the pain anymore and asked for some medication. Enough of the natural breathing crap!

The nurse gave me an injection through my IV. The medication took effect immediately. It was wonderful. I was awake but felt no pain, yet I could feel the labor. Within thirty minutes it wore off and I resumed labor. That routine continued for a few hours, then the doctor put an internal pressure catheter inside of me to monitor how strong my labor pains were.

That procedure was more painful than the labor, but it showed him that my pains were very strong–and one thing was for sure, Travis was not coming out this way. The decision was to do an emergency C-section. They told Jeff because they had to put me under, he would not be able to go into the operating room. We both were very disappointed. He kissed me goodbye and I was off.

I felt bad that he was not able to be in the OR, so going through the doors, I handed my camera to a man with a gown and face mask, "Please take pictures for my husband." He embraced my camera and nodded yes.

As I was being anesthetized, I heard Dr. Moen say to Dr. Rowland, "I think this baby is going to be about eight to nine pounds."

Dr. Rowland said, "Are you kidding? Did you see the size of that woman's stomach? It's going to be at least a ten or twelve pounder."

With that remark, I was out. When I woke up in the recovery room it was in was empty, I had a moment of panic. Where was everyone? Where is my baby? A moment later a nurse walked in, "Everything is fine. You have an eleven pound, thirteen ounce, healthy boy. Let me finish you up and I'll wheel you down to the nursery. Your husband is already down there."

As the nurse wheeled me out I could see Jeff down the hall. Jeff was leaning on his cane and had a big smile. The day had taken a toll on him, but he was a proud, Dad, grinning from ear to ear.

My heart started pounding and uncontrollable tears ran down my face as the nurse picked Travis up and handed him to me. I was a nervous wreck. I never baby-sat when I was younger. I was a tomboy. I was into horses and dancing. I had never changed a real diaper. I was a mother to every stray animal in the neighborhood, but kids scared me to death.

He was so beautiful. I counted all of his fingers and toes. He looked up at me with what looked like blue eyes. He was as bald as they came; just a little peach fuzz. His mouth was moving up and down like a fish out of water. It was like he was saying, "Hey Mom, you're a little tardy with the food. I'm hungry, so get to it."

I had no idea how to breast feed. No one had shown me, and the nurse, sensing my anxiety after a few minutes, said, "I'll feed him for you. You can take the next feeding."

My body was running on pure adrenalin. Even though my abdomen had been sliced open I felt no pain. I walked down to the nursery one last time, pushing the IV pole. I could see that everyone was excited about a new life coming into this world.

I wished my Dad was alive to share in this beautiful moment and that my Mom had recovered enough to see her only grandson. I was glad Jeff's parents were in town and that they came to see him a few hours later. Travis was their only grandchild.

By the time I got back to my room, it was midnight. God had blessed us with a son, Travis Andrew Winans, born August 2, 1985. Just as I closed my eyes, the nurse flipped on the lights, "Hello Mrs. Winans. Coffee, tea or milk?" It was time to feed Travis. The day's events were starting to sink in.

Chapter 10

Reality Sets In

My maternity leave had flown by and Travis was already two months old. Jeff's doctors from Turlock decided to send him to San Francisco to see the world renowned micro vascular surgeon, Dr. Harry Buncke.

Dr. Buncke and his team, which consisted of most of his family members, had the whole fourth floor at Ralph K. Davies Medical Center. Rumor was that he and Dr. Andrews wrote the micro-vascular books when they were surgeons in Vietnam.

After running some tests to evaluate Jeff's injuries, Dr. Buncke said they would like to try and make a new leg. If he went forward with the surgery it would be very invasive and extensive by performing transplants, taking parts of his own body; bones from his hips, nerve and vessels, muscles from his inner thigh, and skin from his upper thighs.

Jeff's response was simple. He looked at Dr. Buncke without batting an eye, "Doc, I don't want to lose my leg, but I also don't want to go through thirty to forty surgeries only to lose the leg anyway. I have a newborn son and I want to be able to run and play with him. If you can help me accomplish that, then I say let's go for it."

They shook hands and we set a date for the first procedure. Jeff would need more blood transfusions and after learning more about AIDS, I re-contacted all of our friends and family to donate blood. I contacted Jeff's parents visiting family in Oregon and let them know what was going on.

The morning of the surgery was tough–especially knowing what he was about to go through. I had to put my trust in God as I prayed over Jeff and kissed him goodbye.

After his initial prep, they took him to the hospital's burn unit. There, they used a special machine to shave the layers of skin off the top of his thighs, which would be used for skin grafts behind the back of his right calf. They put a burn salve and a special clear plastic over his bloody thighs.

Once he was in surgery, they made two-inch incisions in both hips taking bone from each side. They ground up the bone and used it for grafts in the leg. Next, they made a long incision down his left inner thigh and removed the muscle. They told us the inner thigh muscle is normally only used by pro athletes and would not be noticed except for the scar.

From there, they made several more incisions down his leg that ran from just below the left knee down to the top of his ankle. They removed nerves and vessels to be inserted into the right leg and ran a catheter down his spine and enlarged the vessel they had taken. That's the short version. It was hell!

Then something we hadn't planned on happened a few hours later. The transplanted vessel developed a clot. With not enough oxygen and blood flow to keep it working, the inner thigh muscle they had taken from his left leg died.

It was heart wrenching to learn what had happened. I didn't know how much more he could take. Dr. Buncke looked at us with little emotion, "Jeff, there is one other procedure we can do besides amputation. But, we would have to do it immediately."

"I'm listening, Doc."

"We would have to take you back to the burn unit and take more skin, this time from your buttocks. We could take the lattices muscle from your back and try the procedure again. It's one last chance to save your leg Jeff, or we can move forward and amputate now."

Without hesitation, Jeff said, "Like I said before I want to run and play with my son, Doc. I'll try anything to be able to do that."

We were going for it. Jeff looked at me; I smiled and nodded.

Even though the doctors were exhausted, they were pros. They weren't kidding about the wait. They were scrubbing again. I kissed Jeff goodbye, again, and went to the waiting room and prayed. I left a message for Jeff's parents, then called my Mom and made sure she put Jeff back on the prayer line. Later I called Bill and Polly.

Prayer is a powerful thing and God is a maker of miracles. I knew that whatever happened now was in his hands, not mine. Still, it didn't make it any easier.

My back was killing me, but I could endure anything right now knowing what my husband and these doctors were going through. I walked the halls and went to the hospital chapel. I called my office collect, got coffee, put a chair in front of me and made a "make shift" bed in the waiting room. Hours later, the nurse came in to let me know they were bringing Jeff out of OR to recovery. He was alive and everything at that point was working.

They put him in a private isolation room in ICU, so I had to wear a gown and mask to protect him from infection. It was almost too much to bear when I first laid eyes on him after the surgery.

There were tubes of blood coming out of each leg for blood drainage and another tube full of blood coming from his right side. His lower right leg was bandaged. His left lower leg was sliced open from just below the knee all the way to his ankle and sewn up where they extracted the nerve and vessels. His raw bloody thighs and now raw buttock where they had taken his skin for the grafts, were seeping blood and salve.

I bit my lip and kept my composure. If Jeff ever had heart problems, there were no more vessels to steal. Monitors were everywhere. I couldn't let him see what I was feeling inside.

I went over and gently kissed his forehead and whispered, "Hey honey, you made it. I'm here. Travis sends his love and can't wait to see his Daddy. I love you so much."

I was so glad they had him under heavy sedation. The next few days were touch and go, but this muscle transplant seemed to be working.

I was afraid that my job was in jeopardy, so by Sunday afternoon, I had no choice but to leave Jeff and head back to Turlock. I picked

Travis up from Bill and Polly's house. They were close friends with Jeff's parents and took care of Travis whenever I was out of town. He was just waking up from his nap. God, he was so precious and so innocent. He had no idea what was going on. I was thankful for that.

Around two in the morning, I woke up out of a much needed sleep. I looked up and saw the shadow of a very tall man. I grabbed my glasses off the night stand and put them on so I could see. The shadow appeared to look like Jeff but I needed more light. I reached over and turned on the lamp. Oh my God, it was Jeff!

I thought I was dreaming. He was dressed in a tank top, gym shorts and a CBS hat my brother Steve had given him. He was just standing there, staring at me. I sat up in the bed staring back at him. I could hear my heart pounding as I said, "Jeff. Jeff?" It was then I realized then that there was not a mark on his body. No gunshot accident; nothing. What was going on? I was so confused. Once again I said, "Jeff, Jeff!"

I got up out of bed and slowly started toward him when he just disappeared. I thought maybe he had gone into Travis's room so I ran across the hall and tried to turn on the light. It wouldn't come on. I ran over to Travis's crib in the dark and touched him with my fingers. He was sound asleep. I turned around. Jeff was standing in the bedroom doorway. I ran towards him and he disappeared again. I ran down the hall towards the living room calling Jeff's name out again. Am I losing my mind?

Travis woke up from the sound of my voice and started crying. When I tried to turn the hall light on, there was a "force of electrodes" that I can't explain to this day. They were painful, electrocuting me so I couldn't turn the light on. I wouldn't give up. Finally, I said, "Please God help me," as I hit the switch with everything I had. The force was gone and the hall light turned on. I searched the house, but Jeff was nowhere to be found.

My hands wouldn't stop shaking. Confused and dazed, I ran back into Travis's room, picked him up and brought him to bed with me. Trying to stay calm, I decided to keep the night lamp on.

Travis was so cute. He looked over at me and cracked a smile. I smiled back and started rubbing his forehead singing, "Hush little baby don't you cry." He was such a precious gift and blessing. A peace came over me and we fell asleep together.

A few hours later, the phone rang. It was the hospital. They said Jeff had taken a turn for the worse and had gone into cardiac arrest. They were able to revive him, but it didn't look good. Chills ran down my spine. I believe that Jeff had been at the house when he had gone into cardiac arrest. That is why I was able to see him. Could the electricity of the paddles touching his chest as he was being resuscitated, electrocuted my hand?

I didn't have time to think about it now. I looked at the clock. It was four-thirty. Travis was awake from the phone ringing and he was hungry. I called Polly, fed Travis, took a shower, dropped him off at Polly's and headed up to San Francisco.

By the time I got to the hospital, Jeff was a lot more stable. He looked like death, but he was alive. I called Mike and told him what had happened. By mid-afternoon, Jeff seemed to be out of the woods.

I would work during the week and then go up to San Francisco on the weekends, spend a few hours, come home, and get ready to go to work again. I would take Polaroid pictures of Travis so Jeff wouldn't feel left out. He was such a good baby and his presence constantly reminded me how precious life is.

The bills continued to pile up and my employer had not paid any hospital bills except for a few dribbles for the last six months. Money was going out faster than it was coming in. Jeff and I always prided ourselves on our immaculate credit. The credit card companies wouldn't work with us until we were delinquent. Funny how that works; I'll never understand that one.

George Anderson confirmed that the sporting goods store where we bought the gun had lapsed their insurance policy three days before the accident. The gun distributor was our only hope. I wanted to change the law and get a bill passed so that all gun distributors would have to test their guns before distribution, so we went forward with the suit.

Christmas would be here before we knew it. It was Travis's first one. If everything went well, Jeff would be home too. At this point in my life, I don't know what I would have done without my faith. I prayed to God that through all of this, that it would bring Jeff and his parents closer to Him, too.

Two weeks before Christmas, Jeff was able to come home. I got the tree up and decorated. It was a memorable Christmas–one I will never forget. A new year would soon be upon us.

Chapter 11

All About Travis

By February 1986, Jeff had almost fully recovered from the transplants. His rehab, however, was longer than we expected and his recurring infections were still a major problem.

I was spending a lot more time on the road. So Bill and Polly took care of Travis when I was gone. I don't know what I would have done without them as Jeff's parents were constantly traveling and at that time Jeff was not physically capable. Home Health Care came in daily to give Jeff his meds and rehab.

After Travis was born, Jeff's NFL pension only increased $100 to $ 970 per month, but something was better than nothing. We were still trying to find out when his pension would be increased to the larger football disabled pension. At this point we had to rely on Hooper and Alan Page to take care of everything.

The creditors were not working with us anymore. They started calling me at the office. Thank God we had an unlisted number in Turlock. My office manager at my main office in Modesto was wonderful. He never said a word. He just took the messages. It was very embarrassing.

At the end of March 1986, we got the long-awaited letter from Social Security. They had reviewed everything and the judge had approved his Social Security disability. We would receive an additional $600 per month. Now we had to file for Medicare to try to cover some of our future medical bills.

A few days later, I got a call from George's secretary that he needed to see me right away so I went over on my lunch hour.

"Come in Brandi and sit down. I got a letter from your employer. They confirmed that they have filed a lawsuit and are suing you and Jeff personally. They also notified the gun distributor and they have placed a lien on it as well."

I didn't need to be hearing this right now. I was already so distraught, "George, how could they do that?"

"Because it is written in the benefit book now, they have the right to recover their money".

"But it wasn't in there when the gunshot accident happened."

"I know."

"Well how can they sue us personally?"

"Suing you and Jeff personally insures their money. That way they make sure that they get theirs first and if there is any left over, you and Jeff would get the rest, less my attorney fees."

I smiled, "So, you are cutting your attorney fees right?

He just smiled back.

Every time I thought things were getting better, there was a new obstacle in our way. I was not going to let them win. With God's help, we would overcome. I just didn't have a clue how.

On August 2, 1986, Travis had his first birthday. My in-laws were in town and it was fun to plan something with my mother-in-law. We had a number of friends who had small children, so I hired a clown to do tricks and make balloons.

It was a day to remember, because Jeff was there and it was the day Travis took his first steps. He was mesmerized by the clown. He sat in his little chair with his little birthday hat on and little blue bathing suit–in awe while the clown performed tricks.

We only had one major scare when he was thirteen months old. He had a cold and I was on the road. Polly was taking care of him and I stopped by to pick him up on my way home from work. She was holding him when she opened her front door, I could see he wasn't feeling well. As we turned to walk into her living room, his eyes rolled up, and he became motionless.

We rushed him to the convenient care clinic around the corner, where he was diagnosed with bronchitis. The doctor gave us a prescription and told us to take Travis off any other medication. Polly and I both looked at him, "Except for the Tylenol?"

"No, the antibiotics will take care of everything."

I let Travis sleep with us that night and around two in the morning I felt our bed start to shake. I rolled over and saw Travis having a seizure. I picked him up and ran screaming down the hall to the living room where Jeff was watching TV. By that time Travis had stopped breathing and he was burning up. Jeff started CPR and we rushed him to the emergency room.

After he was stabilized, one of the nurses asked us when was the last time he had any Tylenol. They were so angry at us when I told them what the doctor said at the clinic. His fever was so high, they had to put him on ice. They decided to do a spinal to check for meningitis. Jeff and I were so helpless. It was a very humbling experience.

Travis made a full recovery and since Jeff was doing so well, we decided to have Travis's Baptismal, October 13th, 1986. Bear Trilizzio, a longtime friend of Jeff's from his Buffalo Bills days, who is now a pastor in San Diego, did the honors. Bear's new wife, Corrie joined us in the ceremony. Bill and Polly and their son Fritz became Travis's official Godparents that day.

When I ordered his baptismal cake, I didn't know what to have the bakery write on it. Then the Holy Spirit came over me and I knew. It said, "Thank You Father for giving us Travis." It was a beautiful ceremony with a few friends and family, and we baptized him in our Jacuzzi tub outside.

Travis went through a lot before he was even five years old. He barely knew his father because much of the time Jeff lived in a hospital bed somewhere. Travis's temperament and his actions were always kind, gentle and funny. He was a happy child. He had no idea that he was the one who kept both of us going and gave me a reason to keep my faith and hope.

One night, coming home from work I was so tired. It had been a very distressing day, my patience was wearing thin. When I turned on his bedroom light, I just lost it. Travis had drawn all over his bedroom wall. I called him to his room and said angrily "Travis Andrew, did you draw all over this wall?"

He studied it very carefully, looked over at me so proud and said "Yeah Mom, but I could have done a lot better".

I just looked at him and everything that had gone wrong that day became right. My anger and frustrations turned to mush.

Travis always had a mind of his own. He got his independence from both of us. He started picking out his own clothes at three years old. He wore a Superman outfit that Polly had made for him for preschool for almost a year. She knitted him so many outfits, sweaters, etc.

Travis seemed to understand that he couldn't really fly. He just loved the outfit and watched the Superman movies all the time. To this day, Superman is one of Travis's all-time comic heroes.

We always had a lot of fun. I was thankful that he seemed to have a wonderful and loving personality (outgoing, comedic, always on camera and putting on a show), and his Dad's athletic talent.

As much as we tried to include Jeff in whatever we were doing, he tended to alienate himself. Travis was always very forgiving of his father. He knew firsthand what his Dad was going through.

In fifth grade, Travis got interested in playing golf and basketball, and from the time he was ten he was either at a basketball or golf camp. Jeff was still able to play golf so it became one of the few things we could do as a family. By high school, it was all basketball.

It wasn't until Travis was fourteen, that we took our first family vacation. It was at that time that Travis started realizing that I was more than his mother–I was also a woman. As expected , it was more difficult for him to hang with me. He was becoming a young man; hormones raging and all that goes with the transition. He started to grow like a weed. It became awkward for him to talk to me the way he did before. I understood. He watched everything I put on. It wasn't supposed to be sexy. It was almost comical. If I would sing or dance around the house, he would say, "Mom, stop that."

I would come back and say, "Travis, this is our home. I enjoy it and I will dance and sing if I want to". Then he would get this little smile on his face and I knew he was okay.

He was also quite the artist–although by the time he reached high school, he felt being an artist was nerdy. He loved all sports. He tried little league, but switched over to basketball in sixth grade, it became his love, he lived and breathed it. He was the leading scorer for all of Pinellas County in the 2002-2003 season. He had a few games where he scored over 50 points, and he averaged 27.4 points per game.

Coaches from the opposing teams were so impressed with him after some games that they would shake his hand and try to recruit him.

He was the first player to make the 1,000 Point Club at his high school. In May 2007, he was inducted into his High School Hall of Fame and has continued to grow into a man that we are very proud of.

Chapter 12

Twists and Turns

Our lease came up on our rental house and we had an opportunity to buy down the street from where the gunshot accident took place. It had a large corner lot and small three bedrooms, a 1950s style home with angled roofs and lots of glass. A house we could grow into and expand if needed.

We weren't sure if we could qualify, but it was now or never to try. We were able to get an FHA loan with a small down payment. This time we hired the movers. Buying the house took our minds off everything we had been going through and gave Jeff back some dignity.

When Jeff and I were together, we always had either a cat or a dog, or several of them in the house. Sometimes, I would rescue animals in the neighborhood or our cat, "Cat", would bring one home. When I was pregnant, Cat brought home what I thought was someone's hamster. It looked like a hamster so I walked the neighborhood trying to find its home only to find out after I took it to the vet to get its little hernia fixed that cat had brought home a mole.

Farmers kill moles, but this one was so friendly and cute. Jeff was so embarrassed. After a few months, at his insistence, I took him back to the field and let him go, pouring a bag of food down a hole I dug for him.

Another time Cat brought home a very strange bird. A few days later we awoke to this bird singing up a storm. It turned out to be a very expensive rare canary, only mature males of this breed sing. It just so happened that Jeff's friend bred them, and our bird was studded out. Ha.

Jeff seemed to take to the bird, so I bought him a parakeet. We named him Jigger (my Dad's nickname). He loved that bird. We kept his wings clipped. Jeff would sit outside with him on his shoulder on the patio or Jigger would sit on top of his cage. We had him several years. Then, one day, Jigger just flew away. He had forgotten to clip his wings. Jeff was devastated.

By now the lawsuit my insurance company had filed to recover medical expenses was getting ugly. I couldn't believe what they were doing to my family. I was ashamed of myself because I was still working for them, but for now I didn't have a choice. We needed the money. By compromising my principles, I didn't know who I was anymore.

In the midst of this difficulty with my insurance company, another bombshell that we weren't expecting dropped. It was a certified letter from the NFL, saying they were pulling Jeff's disability pension. According to the NFL, the neutral physician they sent Jeff to just before the muscle transplants claimed that he was no longer disabled from football–but from the gunshot accident. The doctor hadn't even looked at his NFL injuries. His concern was only with the gunshot wound, and had reported his findings based on that alone.

They didn't waste any time. Jeff's pension would end the following month. I wondered how people could sleep at night knowing they were literally destroying families–for the almighty dollar. This was more than Jeff or I could emotionally handle.

We didn't know how this would affect our pursuit of his total and permanent disability football-related pension. Surely the arbitration ruling would stand up.

We talked to NFL attorney, Wayne Hooper, who was more confused than we were. Then I called Mickey Yaras at the NFL Players Association and left her a message. I had talked to her before when Jeff was in the hospital and had to postpone his original neutral physician's appointment.

After this last bit of news, I had to get out of the house for a little while. I had so much on my shoulders, but knew I couldn't fall apart in front of Jeff and Travis. I had to be the strong one right now–especially for them.

I felt like I was losing my faith. My resistance was down, I had bronchitis again. This time my doctor put me on an inhaler. Jeff's infections were back. He was constantly in the hospital and our medical bills continued to pile up. As I sat in the Raley's Shopping Center I started to pray.

The answer was clear. I had to stop trying to control everything. I had to let everything go and give everything back to God.

I went home and walked in the front door, "Honey, you are right. We can't do this anymore. I'm going to call a few attorneys and see what we can do to file bankruptcy. Our credit is ruined anyway. The creditors won't leave us alone and refuse to work with us."

Jeff had been after to me to look into filing, but I was too stubborn, thinking I could save the world. I couldn't. As long as I had Jeff and Travis, we could survive anything.

I found an attorney in Modesto, borrowed $750 for his retainer fee and we filed bankruptcy in 1987. We kept our secured debts and let our unsecured debts, hospital and credit cards, go.

The lawsuit for the gunshot accident was still pending. Once it was settled, and if we won, we could take that money and use it to pay off our other debts–well, some of them.

Within a few weeks, my fight and my faith were back. I told Jeff, "We're gonna fight the NFL ourselves. I'll write the letters and you sign them. I won't let them forget what they are doing to us."

"You can't fight them Brandi, they're too big!," he said sarcastically.

"Watch me," I said defiantly.

Jeff thought I was crazy to keep fighting something that he swore we would never win. But after I wrote the letter, he looked at me, shook his head and signed it.

We had the right to appeal every six months. So, every six months we applied. Every six months we were denied.

We hired several attorneys over the years to represent us. It always seemed like they were going to help us fight the NFL, but within a few months, had no more interest.

Jeff would look at me every time we would get denied and almost gloat because we were denied. Every time we got denied I fought back again. He didn't understand that kind of faith. One thing was for sure, the NFL knew who we were.

As time went on Jeff's pride and dignity were squashed. He started to crawl back into the only thing that numbed him–his prescription drugs. I understood, because of the all the surgeries, and the physical and emotional pain he was in. It wasn't long before he was hooked all over again. Only this time it was ten times worse.

I continued to see my shrink whenever I could. Jeff stopped going.

I found a really good male counselor in Modesto who was referred to me by the local Social Security Disability office. Jeff was required to go, and to my surprise, the counselor and Jeff hit it off. Both SSI and NFL psychiatrists and psychologists continued to do more psychological testing on Jeff. His headaches were more severe; his behavior and mood swings more erratic, he had numbness in his arms and hands, and was in constant pain.

The NFL was supposed to pay us back when Jeff was deemed totally disabled from football, but we had never seen a dime for Dr. Berg's bills or any of Jeff's NFL medical bills. I found out through my research on disabled NFL players that at that time, only seven players had ever been given total and permanent disability income from football-related injuries. The players that did receive disability income had gone back to see the same neutral physician they had seen earlier. This tactic was worth a shot.

I called one of the players benefits plan administrators and asked her if Jeff could see Dr. John Becker, the neutral physician that he had seen before. To my surprise, they agreed.

I called Dr. Becker's office and scheduled the appointment. Jeff didn't want to go. "What do you have to lose, except an afternoon," I asked him. After multiple complaints and arguments of why it was a worthless trip, he agreed to go.

After reviewing Jeff's previous records and doing a new evaluation, Dr. Becker agreed that Jeff had continued to deteriorate and was disabled from football due to the degenerative disc disease in his neck and back, and was therefore qualified for total and permanent disability. He also evaluated his ankle and knee.

Still, in the process of evaluating his physical problems, not one doctor had ever examined him for symptoms of multiple concussions or any type of brain injury. This in spite of the fact that Jeff constantly complained to them of severe headaches.

I filed again, and we were back on the NFL board docket. It felt good and this time, we felt there was no way they could not give us back his pension if Dr. Becker's report stated that he was disabled from football–but as always the surprise was on us.

The letter we had been waiting for came; they tabled Jeff for further investigation and sent him to another neutral physician and psychiatrist; anything to keep dragging the claim out.

To make matters worse, I was called to meet with George Anderson, the attorney I had hired to pursue the gun manufacturer and distributor. I didn't know how much more I could take. As I sat down in George's office, I could tell by the look on his face I wasn't going to like it.

"Brandi, your company's attorneys are flying into Modesto to depose you and Jeff."

"Depose us? Why?"

"They want to have a detailed account of Jeff's gunshot accident and the lawsuit we filed with the gun distributor. It's an intimidation tactic," he said calmly.

My anger boiled. "So I have to take more time off of work to come in and talk to their goons from Los Angeles? Screw them, George. Screw them!"

George looked at me very sternly "Brandi, I know how frustrated you are. I know you would like to tell the company to 'stuff it.' I know if you didn't have a young son and a disabled husband to provide for, you would have done it a long time ago. We're almost there, so let's do this and show them that we are not intimidated. Okay?"

"Okay," I replied, staring at his desk. I looked up and said harshly, with tears in my eyes "But George, as soon as this is over and Jeff stops having surgeries, we're out of here. That is if we have anything left with which to leave."

The company I worked for flew in three lawyers from Los Angeles. I had George. The personal lien they had on Jeff and me was for $50,000 and they were asking for $250,000 plus their attorney fees from the potential proceeds of the lawsuit we had filed against the gun distributor. It was everything I could do to maintain being a lady. We didn't back down or let them intimidate us. Now, we waited.

While we were waiting to hear back from my company's attorneys, we got another blow from the NFL board. Jeff's case was tabled again.

His rage was taken out on me. He wanted to quit fighting with them and he was angry at me because I refused to give up. I couldn't. If I did, they would win. Our fight wasn't about us anymore. It was about our family's survival, and we didn't want this to ever happen to anyone else.

I stared at the NFL letter over and over, and then, just snapped. I called George. "Call the gun distributor and tell them we will go away for $500,000 today."

"What?" He said in a frustrated voice. "Brandi we are so close to winning this case. The trial is only six months away."

"George they have postponed the trial date twice."

"I know Brandi, but..."

"You and I both know they can do that until doom's day. Please, just call them and tell them that this is a onetime offer; today only."

George called their attorneys, and to my surprise got through to them and made the offer. After several hours of negotiations, the gunshot case was finally over. They would put the paperwork together for us and have us sign a release.

Jeff was upset with me, but I understood. After all the hell we had been through as a family, and after what he had been through physically, was that all his leg was worth?

I don't know what the end result would have been if we had waited, but I was ready for a nervous breakdown. The money didn't matter. My sanity and the peace our family so desperately needed was what mattered.

My company got their money first, our attorney fees were next, and we walked away with $155,000.

I turned in my resignation, but to my surprise the president of the company called me to say he wouldn't accept it.

I was stunned. "Terry, you just don't get it. Why would you think I would want to stay working for a company that just destroyed my family and my career? How could I possibly go out and recommend your company? I am ashamed that I didn't have the backbone to resign sooner."

"Well, I'm not going to accept your resignation for now. I'll put you down as taking a leave of absence. You'll always have a job here."

"Thanks Terry, but as far as I'm concerned, I'd rather starve than work for this company again. I just hope and pray that this never happens to anyone else."

Terry was a good man. I watched him climb up the ranks as one of my former bosses and what they did to me was way out of his control. He could only offer to keep my job open.

Bankruptcy court was next. Because of the bankruptcy, the $155,000 we received from the gunshot case had to be placed in a trust account with our assigned trustee. The big question of the day was whether we were going to be allowed to keep it or was it going to have to go to our creditors?

To our surprise, none of our creditors showed up at the courthouse to claim anything–not even the hospitals. Our attorney explained what happened with the lawsuit and my company not paying our medical bills and pleaded with the judge to rule that this money was needed as income to keep the family afloat due to Jeff's physical disabilities.

The judge had sympathy. The $155,000 was exempt from the creditors. The bankruptcy was officially over and done. The gunshot case was settled. Now we had a chance to start over.

Chapter 13

The Inheritance

With everything that happened in California behind us, we decided to move back to Florida, where I grew up on St. Pete Beach. Jeff had been surgery free for almost nine months. My health had deteriorated over the past few years. Partly due to all the stress I was under and partly due to the agricultural town in which we lived. I had developed acute bronchitis through all of this, and my family doctor advised me to leave the area as well.

We came home to Florida for my 20th Class Reunion in July 1988, when Travis was almost three years old. My Mom was so excited because it was only the second time she had seen Travis. I was excited because I had actually gotten Jeff to go. He rarely went to functions and it meant a lot that he was with me and we were there as a family. The fact that he would go to my Class Reunion was a big bonus.

The reunion was so much fun and I was able to introduce Jeff to some of my old classmates. He seemed to enjoy himself, too. It's always fun to see how we all age; some more than others. Ha. Where was I on the totem pole?

We decided to look at some real estate. It's very hot and humid in Florida in July. After agreeing to look at some houses, Jeff was apprehensive and his temper was short-fused. He would give me the Black Eye stare every time he stepped outside of the hotel room. We decided Travis and I would be the real estate look-e-loos and then take him on the ones that we thought he might like.

You could look at Jeff and he would start to sweat. He would take two shirts with him when we went out and a large hand towel to wipe the sweat that bubbled up on his forehead and neck.

He had a phobia for being around anyone he didn't know. Because Jeff was a big man, he assumed that everyone was looking at him. This kind of behavior escalated after he left football.

After looking in the beach area, we decided that the schools we wanted Travis to attend were in the North East area of St. Petersburg. Jeff's only requirement was that if we moved here it had to be on the water. Okay, we were on the water...I did my part.

We found a beautiful three year old waterfront home, near the schools we wanted Travis to go to. It had an open floor plan, high vaulted ceilings, a beautiful oak kitchen, split bedroom plan, Jacuzzi and a dock. It appeared to be well built by the contractor/owner.

We signed a contract and put a deposit down. The silver Volvo station wagon we bought while there could stay in the garage until we returned in October.

Jeff actually got excited about the move. At first he didn't want to move back to Florida, but with my bronchitis, I knew I couldn't stay here. I was starting to feel some of my stress was being lifted. I really felt this would be a positive turning point in our lives. We decided to keep our house in California and do a lease option with some friends we knew.

We had four garage sales the last month we were in Turlock and sold almost everything we owned so we could start fresh. Travis and I flew out from Oakland and Jeff and "Cat" came a few weeks later in the U-Haul truck.

It was fun to buy new furniture and Travis had the most fun picking out his room. We purchased some exercise equipment after the lawsuits and decided to open up a franchise called Trim N Tone on St. Pete Beach. My other brother George, a carpenter and a few of his friends helped us build out the store.

By November of 1988 a month after we moved into the new house, another certified letter from the NFL arrived. Jeff stopped getting excited.

"Honey, aren't you going to you open it," I asked.

"Why, so I can be disappointed again?"

He gave me one of those here we go again looks and opened the letter. It was the news we had been wanting so long for, but not the news we wanted to hear. This time Jeff was classified as total and permanently disabled, but non-football related. The monthly pension was the same as we had been getting before; $870 plus $100 for Travis.

Dr. Becker had just stated that he was disabled from football due to back injuries. It wasn't right. I contacted the NFL Disability Benefits division. They said the Board decided it should be non-football related because of the gunshot accident

"The gunshot accident was after we won arbitration with Sam Kagel, July 1984," I said. "Jeff was disabled from football in 1981–way before the November 1984 accident. This should have no bearing on his NFL disability pension."

They didn't see it that way. They saw the gunshot accident as a way of not paying Jeff what he deserved. Eight years of fighting the NFL, four more years of fighting for hospital benefits, filing bankruptcy, and leaving the job I had planned to be with the rest of my life, I had no more fight in me.

The $970 a month would help put food on the table and gas in the car. Maybe later my fight would come back, but not now.

For now, I had to concentrate on our Trim N Tone Salon and providing for our family. The concept of letting the machines tone your muscles while you relaxed got a good response. The exercise machines were easy to use and we were drawing in a few clients. We bought a facial machine that massaged and toned the muscles in the face and I got certified to help enhance the business. I also joined the local beach chamber and hosted a few chamber mixers at the salon. I worried sometimes that my back wouldn't hold up. It would go out on me without warning.

Travis was in pre-school and for now my mother's back had healed, so we were able to have her over more.

Late one night, I got a call from my brother Steve while he was on location. "I got a call from an attorney on my answer machine from

North Carolina that Uncle Marvin (Mom's brother) had died and wanted Mom to know. Will you call her for me?"

He gave me the attorney's name and phone number. I called Mom and told her about Uncle Marvin. There had been a major falling out with her family and she hadn't seen any of her family members since 1968.

"Why are they calling me," she asked. "I can't go to the funeral. I guess I could send a card."

"Mom, don't analyze, just call the attorney tomorrow, Okay? Maybe you and the Byrds can reunite and make-up. They are your family no matter what. Let the past go, Mom. You can't bring it back. Besides, Uncle Marvin didn't even have anything to do with your feud with your Mom. If you would like me to call for you, I'll be happy to."

"You're right Brandi, I'll call in the morning."

The next morning I got a call from Mom. She was very upset.

"What's wrong Mom?"

"I called the attorney this morning."

"Why are you so upset? What did Uncle Marvin die of?"

"It wasn't Uncle Marvin who died," Mom said.

"Then who was it?" Uncle Marvin was the only Marvin I knew. I didn't understand.

She started to cry. "He was my brother's son, Marvin, III. We need to talk. Can you come over right away? There are a lot of things that you and Steve don't know about."

"Sure Mom, I'll be right over."

After I arrived at her apartment, Mom proceeded to tell me that she had been adopted. Her father was sixty-nine years old when she was born. Her mother was fifty. She was a miracle, but not planned. She was born into the Rhew family and had two older brothers who were twenty-eight and twenty-six years older. They both were killed in a hurricane in 1928. Her father died six months after she was born and her mother took ill when she was five, and could no longer care of her, so she was placed in an orphanage in Durham, N.C.

The family I knew (the Byrd Family) as Mom's family, knew her Mom's real Aunt, and when my mother's mother died, not long after she was in the orphanage, they adopted her–or so she thought. She took on their last name of Byrd.

What she told me next was about why she was so upset. When she was a teenager, she had seen a young man named Marvin. She was told he was some distant cousin. She felt very drawn to him every time she saw him. He always looked at her as if he wanted to say something, but never did.

This morning, she found out that Marvin Rhew II, the man she saw as a teen, was actually her half-brother. He had one son named Marvin Rhew III, who died with a brain aneurysm a few months back. He was Mom's nephew–a nephew she never knew about.

This nephew, who owned a large septic tank company in Durham, didn't have a will and never had any children. His wife had died years before, and Mom was the sole survivor of his estate. The estate was worth about three million dollars. There was a lot more to the story, maybe I'll write about it in another book, but bottom line, she was a millionaire!

I never knew what she had been through as a child. My heart poured out for her and I realized how all those years she covered it up. I started to understand her animosity towards the Byrd family, but always thought they had her best interest at heart. For the first time in my life,I understood her insecurities...

We sat on the couch, laughed and cried all at the same time. It really was a miracle. After all those years, she finally knew who her family was and that was way more important than the money she would inherit.

Chapter 14

Pennsylvania Avenue

Once we were settled into our new house, Jeff decided Travis was old enough to have a puppy. After much debate about what kind of dog we would get, Jeff decided he wanted an English Mastiff.

He found an ad in the paper and spent a good amount of time on the phone with the breeder, and the next thing I knew I was driving to Brooksville, Florida, located about two hours from the house.

The minute I saw twelve week old, Cherokee Alantes Bodacious, I was in love. He came over and looked up at me with those big brown eyes and it was all over. The look on Jeff's and Travis's face when I walked in the door with him was priceless. He was a welcome addition to the family and "Cat" had a new friend. I had no idea that this puppy would grow up to be 225 pounds of love.

A few months after we moved we started having a lot of problems with it. It literally was falling apart before our eyes. The back patio split almost into where the in-ground Jacuzzi was located. More cracks appeared in the master bedroom, master patio area, and the garage.

After having a building inspector over to look at the house, we contacted the owner and told him that we were no longer interested in purchasing it and wanted our $7,500 back. He responded by giving us a thirty-day notice to move out–without a refund. We hired an attorney who thought we had a good case and started to look for a new place to live.

We learned through our research, and by me knocking on our neighbor's doors and telling them our dilemma, that this was the first house the owner had ever built. The dirt he used under the house foundation was literally a bunch of garbage. The house was settling and creating all the cracks in the house. It was a real money pit.

My brother Steve lived around the corner. He and Jeff seemed to have resolved their differences for now and had their eye on a house about a mile away on the open bay. There was no way we could afford to buy a house. We had just come out of bankruptcy and couldn't get a loan here for two years. Plus, we had rented our California house for two years.

Neither Jeff nor Steve paid any attention. Jeff called the realtor. The seller was asking $214,000. Despite my opinion, Jeff set an appointment for us to look at it. About an hour before we were to meet her there, the realtor called and cancelled due to illness. Jeff was very disappointed and put his grumpy face on. I decided to get out of the house and go to the grocery store.

As I drove by the house we were to see, I saw that there was a small red car in the driveway. I turned around and went back. I thought it was the realtor. I realized the best way to get Jeff back to reality was to show him the house. Then he would realize that we couldn't afford it and move on to something else. I knocked on the front door and an elderly well-dressed lady and a young girl answered the door. I introduced myself and told her who I was and what had happened.

"Well shoot, I'm the owner, this is my granddaughter. Who can show the house any better than I? Come on in…"

As we walked through the house, I told her our saga: the gunshot accident, the bankruptcy, and how Jeff used to play pro football.

I told her what had happened with the house we were in. I was expecting her to say, "Too bad you're not able to buy this now." Instead she said, "I really like you and I am dying to meet your husband. I don't need the money. I'll be happy to finance the house for you".

My mouth dropped open. I wasn't sure what I was hearing.

"I'm sorry Mrs. Knight, could you repeat that please?"

"Bring your husband over this afternoon to look at the house. If he likes it, I'll be happy to finance the house for you at 10% interest for three years until you can get another loan. Please, call me Millie."

I went on to the grocery store and came home. Jeff was still in a terrible mood–pouting like a little kid. He acted like this whenever he didn't get his way. After unloading the groceries, I calmly said, "I saw your house today."

"What house?"

"The one we were supposed to see this morning."

I told him what happened. "It needs a lot of work. It has green shag carpet and nothing has been updated."

I don't think he heard anything past we could see it this afternoon. I didn't mention what Millie said about the financing. A few hours later, we were back in the house with another realtor who was filling in for the sick one. I hadn't seen Jeff's face light up, like it did that afternoon, in a very long time. He loved that the house sat on the open bay with a 212 foot dock and boathouse. We made an appointment with Millie's realtor for the following day, to write the offer.

Paul, Millie's realtor appeared to be very polished. He took us into the conference room and took out a blank contract. Jeff stood up, walked over, took his Super Bowl ring off his finger and laid it down in front of the Realtor on the conference table.

"Paul, I want this house. What do I have to do to get it?"

I had to contain myself as my mouth dropped to the floor. I was ready to choke him! All of the negotiating power we had just went out the window and down the street.

"Mr. Winans, I work for the seller, Mrs. Knight, and I'm afraid that anything you say to me has to be related to her."

Needless to say, we paid almost full price for the house. Millie was a shrewd businesswoman. The house had been on the market a long time. Like she said, she didn't need the money. She saw this as an opportunity to sell the house, finance it at 10% interest, and if we weren't able to sell our property in California, by the time we had our closing in December 1989, we would forfeit $20,000 of any proceeds or profit.

We planned to rent her house for six months, until we could close. We had to figure out how we would come up with the down payment. We ended up paying $2,000 to get the renters in California to leave. They had only been in the house six months. It worked out, because Turlock was booming and we ended up having a bidding war on the house. It sold in days. I always felt it was through God that we bought the house we would eventually live in for seventeen years. God was in control. This was where we were supposed to be. Only he knew what our future would hold.

Chapter 15

Along Came a Spider

The fitness salon we had opened was doing okay, but because of my back and neck problems, and Jeff having more infections, I had to hire a manager to help me. I started losing business and had mixed emotions about what to do. Jeff and I thought this business would do well or we wouldn't have invested $80,000 in the equipment.

June 1989, shortly after we moved into our new house, Jeff came down the hall into the living room while I was cleaning and motioned for me to turn off the vacuum. I looked up and saw he was white as a sheet and was sweating profusely.

"Honey, I don't feel very well. I'm going to drive myself to the hospital."

"What's wrong?"

"I don't know, but this is really starting to hurt."

Jeff pointed to a tiny yellow puss mark that had a red ring around it on the backside of his right forearm. His arm was very warm to the touch, and he felt like he was running a fever.

"I'll drive you, honey," I offered.

I grabbed my purse and drove to the closest emergency room about fifteen minutes away. By the time we got there, he was fading. They put him on a gurney from the car and wheeled him to the emergency room while I filled out all the paperwork. I noticed when they were putting him on the gurney, that his right arm had started to swell.

I filled out the paperwork and waited. A few minutes later, the nurse came out and said I could see him as soon as he was stabilized.

"What's wrong with him," I asked.

"We're not sure Mrs. Winans, but his white count is off the charts and is still climbing."

I asked her about the small puss mark on his arm.

Puzzled, she asked, "How small was it?

"Small."

"Not anymore. His arm keeps swelling. It is extremely red and it's so hot, it's starting to blister."

"Blister?"

"Yes, he may have had been bitten by a poisonous spider, a Brown Recluse, when he was working in the yard. We are going to run some more tests and have called an infectious specialist to look at him. You should be able to go back soon."

"Thank you for the update."

My emotions ran deep as my mind wandered back to the day of the gunshot accident. Had we gone through all of this to lose him now?" When I was finally able to go back and see him, sweat was pouring off his body. The nurse wasn't kidding. His arm was huge and fiery red with little water blisters already raised all over his arm. I stood there so helpless.

He looked at me, "Brandi, get me my wallet." I walked over and pulled it out from his pants pocket. "Look inside, the right side."

I opened up the right side of his wallet and there was a newspaper clipping with a poem called "To Remember Me." The poem was about how he wanted me to remember him when he died. Tears were running down my face as I read this very moving poem.

He looked me in the eye, his body trembling with emotion. "Please Brandi, Please do this for me if anything happens, Please!"

"Of course I will, honey, but we aren't going to have to worry about it. You're going to be fine. Let's just let the doctors do their thing. They called in some specialists. Steve is going to pick Travis up from school, so don't worry about anything right now."

A peace came over him and he settled down, until the nurse came in and told me I had to wait outside in the waiting room. After arguing that he didn't want to be alone, I lost the battle, and was put back in the emergency waiting room.

On the way back, I asked her if he was going to be all right. Her face said it all. We've never seen anything like this before. His fever is rising and we're going to take him for some more tests. We will do everything we can".

"What do you mean?"

"If we can't get his fever and white count under control, we could lose him."

"Oh God." I wasn't expecting to hear that answer. I went into the waiting room bathroom and started to pray. By the time I came out and sat down, several other people had come in. I realized that we all have a story to tell. Why were they there? Where did they come from? I decided to pray for them, too.

Finally a nurse came out and told me they were going to move Jeff up to ICU. His temperature was still rising, his white count was still dangerously high and he was septic. She handed me all of his belongings in a white plastic bag. I thought to myself, is this all I am going to take home?

"You can join him as soon as we get him into his room. You'll have to wear a cap and gown. The nurse will get them for you. We called in a second infectious doctor. In the meantime, we're going to wrap his arm and put him on ice."

I called Steve and told him what was happening. He said he would take Travis home and stay with him. They put Jeff on an infectious ICU status. When I asked why, they said it could be streptococcus.

"What's that," I asked.

She told me that was what killed Jim Henson.

When I walked into Jeff's room, they were trying to start an IV. The nurse was frustrated and couldn't get it in his hands or arms. He had had so many previous surgeries that his veins had collapsed again. The nurse went out to call in a doctor to make an incision on the upper left side of his chest in the artery by his heart. It wasn't the first time Jeff had to have this procedure. Because it was an incision, only a licensed doctor could do the procedure.

I kept praying, asking God for more strength. I had learned one thing over these last few years; not to ever be afraid to ask God for help. It was the only way I could keep some sort of sanity. Just when I thought I couldn't take anymore, there would be a short calm. I was hoping it would come soon.

After watching Jeff go through so much pain, I knew I could go through it, too. His arm was now so big and purple red with tons of blisters that I thought it was going to explode.

They concluded that he had been bitten by a Brown Recluse spider but they couldn't get the antibiotics to kick in. If they didn't start to work soon, he could have a heart attack and die.

At least the pain medication they had given him was working and he was getting some much needed relief. At nine o'clock in the evening they threw me out. It was hard to leave, but I knew I had to get home to Travis. The nurse on duty promised me I could call anytime and get updates. She assured me that she would keep an eye on him for me and call me if there were any changes.

Travis was in bed when I got home. Steve was watching TV. He was to leave on location in the morning so I had to find someone else to pick Travis up if necessary.

The next few days were touch and go. Jeff was miserable. I had never seen anything like this before. His arm was still huge. The blisters had turned to pussy yellow and some had started to scab. The third day they found an antibiotic that started to work. The antibiotics were so powerful that the name Jeff was given before, when he was on the "elephant antibiotics" came back. Jeff was known as the Elephant Man again. I didn't care what they called him, I just wanted him out of the hospital and home.

It's funny when a crisis hits, the things that mean the most always stand out–the value of family and the power of God. With those in mind, anything is possible and hope is never far away.

Five days later, Jeff was home. Unfortunately, his home stay didn't last. Two days after returning home, he took another turn for the worse. Although the swelling in the arm was almost gone, the ugly residue of the blisters and infection were not.

This time Jeff wanted to go to Blake Hospital in Bradenton and be with doctors he knew and trusted. Upon arriving, we got him settled into a room and more tests. His white count was climbing again, so they started him on a different antibiotic finally and got the infection under control again.

The third day at Blake, Jeff called me at work. "You won't believe what I did this morning."

"What?"

"I swallowed my bridge."

"You did what?"

Jeff had a three-tooth gold bridge that had come loose a week before he ended up in the hospital from the spider bite. We had scheduled a dentist appointment, but we both had forgotten that the bridge was loose. During his breakfast that morning, he had swallowed it. They had to take him for ex-rays to see where it was in his system. They would have to do that every day until it passed. Yes, you know where.

By the third week, while Jeff was still in the hospital, the bridge passed. Three days later Jeff was able to finally go home. Another miracle had happened. Thank you, Jesus.

Chapter 16

Jeff's Amputation

Since Jeff's spider bite, things had been going very well. August 2, 1989, we celebrated Travis' fourth Birthday. My Mom, both my brothers and a few friends helped us celebrate. Mom bought Travis a small ATV and he had a blast driving it all over the property. Steve got him a remote controlled car and he put our hamster in it (who either liked it or was scared stiff), and drove the car all over the house.

My brother George and his wife, Pearl, brought over a Batman birthday cake. It was rare for all of us to be together, because one of us was always away somewhere, so this day was special. It was a great way to celebrate everything.

Then, September 1989, a month after Travis's birthday, Jeff's leg became infected again. He had been surgery-free for almost a year and now he had to face several operations.

Following his trip back to Bradenton and Blake Hospital, after almost four emotional and traumatic years, he decided to go forward and have his right leg amputated just below the knee–what they called a BK. October 8, a few days before Jeff's thrity-seventh Birthday, we flew out to California for the surgery.

With the costs incurred treating all the previous infections, our little bit of savings was being depleted rapidly. The amputation would entail a long recuperation and later a fitting for a prosthetic.

Jeff wanted Dr. Harry Buncke at Ralph K Davies Medical Center in San Francisco to do the surgery. We decided that all three of us would go, and would stay at his parent's house in Turlock, about eighty miles east of San Francisco.

A few days after our arrival, Jeff and I met with Dr. Buncke and his team for the consultation and blood work. I made some calls to get more blood donated and the surgery was scheduled.

Jeff called Bear in San Diego, (the pastor who baptized Travis) and asked him to come up and be there for the surgery. I knew if Jeff asked Bear to be there, he was scared. Bear was there in a heartbeat.

The 1989 World Series would be in town in a few days and would be played at Candlestick Park, so downtown San Francisco was already getting very congested.

The night before his surgery, we had a nice family dinner at Jeff's parents. After dinner, I caught Jeff's mother, Janice, upstairs in his bedroom and invited her to come with us for the surgery. I told her I didn't want to be alone, I needed someone to be with me and I would like it to be her. She had only been to visit Jeff in the hospital once since the gunshot accident.

She started to cry, "Thank you Brandi, he's your husband, but he's my son. I would love to go."

We hugged each other for the first time in a long while. Janice was not a maternal person, not touchy-feely like me. I loved her and tried to respect the way she was. I was glad I made the decision to ask her. I knew it was important for Jeff, too, and I knew she would not go unless she felt that she was needed.

The next morning, after we arrived at the hospital, Dr. Buncke called Jeff into his office. He seemed excited.

"Jeff, I have some great news. We don't have to do the BK. There is still enough healthy tissue to be able to do a Symes."

"What's a Symes Doc?"

"It's where we only remove the foot and develop a stump like a peg leg. That way if there is an emergency you could get out of bed and travel much easier."

Jeff was devastated.

Dr. Buncke looked puzzled. "Jeff, what's wrong? I thought you would be happy?"

"Doc, I have mentally prepared for the BK not a Symes. It's like playing football. You have to mentally prepare for the game. Well today is my game day in the OR and I want the BK Okay?" He got very emotional. "No BK, No surgery," and walked out of his office.

Janice and I were outside in the hall with Bear. As we walked over to Jeff, he held his hands up and said, "I have to be alone right now. Please." He turned around and walked down the hall.

"Let's see what Dr. Buncke said," I offered

After finding out, Bear said "Let me go talk to him. You and Janice go get a cup of coffee."

About an hour later, Janice and I were in the waiting room when Jeff and Bear came in. Jeff decided to go through with the surgery and Bear prayed with him. Jeff's surgery had to be done in two stages. Stage one today and stage two a few days later. Jeff would have about a two to three week stay in the hospital.

Jeff and Bear had been estranged for a while after being so close when Jeff played at Buffalo. I was glad he came for this very serious surgery.

Several hours later, Dr. Buncke came out. The first amputation was done. Jeff was doing fine and we could see him after recovery.

We saw him briefly. He was pretty out of it, and soon it was time to leave and head back to Turlock. Bear had to fly back to San Diego. We hugged him and said goodbye. I promised him I would keep him abreast of everything. It was a somber ride home. Janice and I hardly said two words. It had been a very hard day for her, and what do you say after her son and my husband's foot has just been amputated?

Travis was staying at his godparent's house; I gave Janice a hug and went right to bed so I could be back at the hospital the next morning. I didn't want Jeff to feel he was there by himself and it helped me keep my sanity to be with him.

I followed this routine for several days. I would get to the hospital around ten and leave every afternoon by four o'clock. That way I would miss a lot of the traffic going back across the Bay Bridge.

On my way home, October 16, I realized how exhausted and stressed out I had become. It was strange, but just as I was thinking how stressed I was, a little bird said, "Why don't you take the day off tomorrow?" I thought yeah, why I don't take the day off tomorrow.

Then the guilt set in. I should be with Jeff. Then the little birdie said it again "You need a day off. You are exhausted." I thought okay, I'll ask my in-laws to go.

At dinner that evening, I said I was going to take the day off, spend some time with Travis and go to my friend's birthday party.

"Why don't you guys go see Jeff," I asked.

Glenn and his brother Dale both said, "No, the World Series is in town. There's too much traffic for us".

"I know Jeff would love to see you. Well, at least call him tomorrow, please?"

I was still feeling guilty about not going, but once again, the little birdie said, "Just take the day off." I decided to listen. The next morning I took Travis to the park. We had a really nice day with his godparents and my in-laws.

Glenn called Jeff and around a quarter to four as I left to go meet my friends who were having a birthday dinner for Bill Trubitsky. I arrived at the restaurant and we ordered a bottle of wine. We just started to break bread when everything in the restaurant started shaking. We were sitting next to a large aquarium so we decided to go outside.

I was living in Los Angeles when the 1972 earthquake hit. But we didn't think this one was major. In fact, we were joking around outside.

Bill said "I think this is a 6.0."

I said, "No I think it's a 6.5."

Another friend, Bev, was saying it was a 7.0. We weren't really taking it very seriously. When the ground stopped shaking, we went back inside and changed tables. Tony, the owner of the restaurant came out from the kitchen. His face was white as a sheet.

"Hey Tony, we need another bottle of wine."

He just looked at us, speechless; something was terribly wrong.

Seeing the expression on his face I asked, "Tony, what's wrong?"

His voice cracked as he got the words out of his mouth. "We just had a major earthquake and part of the Bay Bridge fell in. They don't know how many people were on the bridge or if there are any casualties, and they aren't sure where the fault is located."

Nothing was funny anymore. I got up out of the booth, ran to the pay phone to call my in-laws and the hospital. All the phones lines were down. I grabbed my purse and ran to my car. All I could thing about was Travis and Jeff and my in-laws. Were they okay? Where else did it hit? The radio stations were trying to assess what happened. I drove like a crazy woman, screeching the tires as I pulled into my in-laws driveway, got out and ran into the house.

Everyone was so calm in the living room and watching the news on TV. I was still a crazy woman. With my eyes glued to the television screen, I slowly started to calm down. I asked Glenn if they had any damage. There was very little, mainly the pool.

The news on the television said the earthquake hit on the San Andreas Fault near San Jose. That meant that San Francisco was hit hard. I ran to the kitchen phone and tried to call the hospital again. All the lines were still down. I was starting to panic when I saw Travis come around the corner and into the kitchen. He ran over and greeted me with a big hug and smile.

"Hi Mommy."

I bent down and picked him up. "Hi Mr. T," I replied, smiling back at him.

All I wanted to do was hold him as tight as I could. I walked back to the living room holding T. I felt strange that I was the only one upset. Jeff was their only son and we didn't know if he was dead or alive.

The damage we were watching on TV was devastating. The Bay Bridge had definitely collapsed. Then it hit me like a lead balloon–if I had followed my regular routine, I would have been on the bridge at the time it collapsed. That little birdie may have saved my life. For the first time, I realized that the sixth sense was Jesus, directing us and protecting us.

The Holy Spirit came all over me. I had never been as blessed as I was at that moment. But what about Jeff? Was he alive? I had to keep the faith.

Trying to keep busy, I decided to do some much-needed laundry. Travis followed me out to the garage. As I put the clothes into the washer, I looked over at him. He had a very somber look on his face. His bottom lip started to quiver and then he just started to cry.

I ran over to him and picked him. "Honey, what's wrong?"

"I don't know Mommy, I don't know, I got scared. I love you Mommy. I'm glad you are home."

"I'm glad I'm home, too. In fact, if you want to, you can sleep with me tonight, okay? Oh, buy the way, Daddy sends you his love. He can't come to the phone right now, but as soon as he can we'll let you say hi."

"Okay, Mommy."

I had to be strong especially for Travis's sake. For the next three days, all we could do was watch the news on TV–no phones, no communication. Jeff's sister, Shari, worked at a hospital in Sunnyvale, near San Jose and was able to find out the next day that Jeff was alive. The hospital was on generators, and she was able to get word to him that we were all fine.

However, no one was allowed in San Francisco unless they had proof that they lived there. Two days later, I was finally able to reach my mother. She had been worried sick. My brother had called from a shoot he was doing on location in Pennsylvania. On the fifth day after the earthquake, I was able to get in to San Francisco to see Jeff.

I was anxious and the drive seemed to take forever. As I opened the door to his private room, I could see a large crack in the wall and places where the pieces of the dry-wall had been. The quake hit so hard, it unlocked the wheels on his bed leaving him helpless, rolling him all over his room banging into walls. The force jerked the IVs out of his arm and took him on a very bumpy ride. He was lucky. It could have been a lot worse.

While I was there, I was able to speak with Dr. Buncke who told us he decided to stay on schedule and operate the next day for the second stage of the amputation. At this surgery, they would make a flap with the excess skin to go over the area where they amputated.

The operation was a success. Jeff was weak and in a lot of pain, but he was out of danger and a few days later, it was time for Travis and me to fly back to Florida.

We had a safe flight home. It was good to sleep in my own bed again. The next morning I got Travis off to pre-school. Returning to the house, I started sorting through the stacks of mail. All of a sudden, I just lost it. I started to cry uncontrollably. Three weeks of pent up emotion exploded. The realization hit me again that God had saved my life the day I decided to take the day off, and that truth strengthened my faith more than ever before.

A few weeks later, Jeff was able to come home. Travis and I picked him up at the airport. He was on crutches and very thin, but he was alive and that was all that mattered.

While unpacking his things, I found a letter that he had written to Travis on the back of a US-Air menu. It was very emotional and moving as he described to Travis what he had been through, and how much he loved him.

We closed on the Pennsylvania Avenue house, December 1989. It was our anniversary present to each other. We had thirty days to come up with the rest of the money we owed Millie. New Year's Eve was quite the celebration. We had so much to be thankful for.

Chapter 17

Another Decision

For a while things were pretty good. But my lower back problems continued to haunt me. The economy was slowing down and business at the shop had slowed down a lot. I couldn't afford to keep my manager, so after talking it over we decided to close the salon.

Looking for work that would allow me to have a flexible schedule, I decided to go to real estate school and get my license. I interviewed with several companies and chose an ERA company called Lambrecht and Associates. Carl Lambrecht and Chris Christian seemed very excited to have me come aboard. All I had to do now was pass my exam.

After completing the real estate school I scheduled my exam in Orlando. There was a lot on my plate, and I had to pass this exam. Our family depended on it. I was hoping that I wouldn't get the math exam. Of course, that's the exam I got and it was tough. As I turned in my paperwork, the gal asked me if I wanted to pay an extra $20 and find out if I passed.

"No thank you".

"Are you sure? It will take about three weeks otherwise" she said.

"That's all right. Thanks for asking though."

I couldn't tell her I didn't have an extra $20 to spend, plus I couldn't handle any more rejection if I failed the exam. A few weeks later, Travis and I were at my Mom's house when Jeff called and said "Your paperwork from the state came. Do you want me to open it?"

I said no. Then I called him back and said, "OK, open it up" I've got to know. I can't keep running from it."

He opened it up. There was silence.

"Jeff, come on tell me, did I pass or didn't I?"

"Congratulations honey, you passed"

I was so excited the neighborhood could have heard me shout for joy. I needed that reinforcement to boost my confidence. I called Carl Lambrecht and went into his office to fill out my paperwork.

As I sat down with him, he shook my hand and said, "Congratulations, Brandi and welcome aboard. We just need to go over a few things and then we can have you fill out the paperwork."

"That sounds great, Carl."

"Brandi, it's important for you to have realistic expectations about being in the real estate business. It's going to take you a while to build your business. We have some floor time, but you will have to market yourself for it to grow. It will take you at least 6-12 months to do that – which means you need to plan on not having any income for that amount of time. Do you and Jeff have enough in your savings to do that?"

My bubble burst. I hadn't thought that it would take that long to start earning any money. We were broke. We had about $1,200.00 in our checking account. We had put almost everything we had into the salon and the closing on the house. Somehow, I thought I would be getting a draw against my commissions. It didn't work like that.

I smiled back at him, "No Problem Carl. When can I get started?"

"I'll let Chris know that you are here. He will get you a desk and you can start classes tomorrow."

"Classes?"

"Yes, you have to go through our orientation and training before you can officially start."

My heart sank. I thought, Okay Lord, I need another miracle. Jeff has put up with me going to real estate school. What am I going to tell him now? Let's see, I could say, "Hi honey, I got my desk today, and it's only going to be six to twelve months before we have any income."

We had been able to sell a few pieces of our equipment to another fitness salon. The most expensive stuff was worthless to anyone so we gave it away and took a loss.

I thought of asking my mother, but decided not to ask her. I had to keep my faith. God is always a God of the last minute, and so far he had somehow pulled us through.

With all those thoughts running through my mind, I thanked Carl for hiring me and simply said, "Great Carl, I'll see you and Chris in the morning".

The Symes amputation Jeff had in San Francisco, had worked for a while; then just like before, Jeff developed more infections. Dr. Buncke had been wrong. From his ankle to just below the knee, Jeff was having major circulation problems.

Jeff went to Bradenton to see an understudy of Dr. Buncke's, who now practiced there, to have some more tests run. The results were not good. To prevent the recurring infections from coming back, they strongly recommended Jeff move forward and do the BK (Below Knee) amputation.

Neither one of us was prepared for this. It seemed like everything was falling apart all over again. His doctor in Bradenton recommended a doctor from St. Petersburg named Dr. Brandies and we made an appointment to see him. He confirmed the BK was necessary. He and Jeff decided to schedule the surgery as soon as the infection was under control.

The morning of the surgery, I dropped Travis off to school at St. Petersburg Christian School and drove to Bradenton. Jeff had taken a cab down the night before so he could get his work-up done. When I got to his room he was surprisingly very cheerful, but I could tell he wanted to get it over with. That was a good sign, because I knew it meant that he was mentally prepared.

I gave him a kiss, sat down and started to rub his arm. He reached over and touched my hand. We hadn't been getting along, but right now we were like crazy glue stuck to each other – never to be separated again. It felt good.

Before I knew it they were ready for him. By now he was a little groggy. He squeezed my hand and I kissed him goodbye.

For some reason, I was worried about this one. Jeff's nine lives had come and gone many times over. I went to the hospital chapel and prayed. The surgery seemed to go on forever. It was mid afternoon when the nurse came in and said, "Mrs. Winans?

"Yes"

"Dr. Brandies asked that I take you into the conference room. He will be in a few minutes".

"Thank You."

She took me into a very small room with cold blank walls. A few minutes later, Dr. Brandies came in and sat down in the chair in front of me. As he shook my hand he said, "Hi Mrs. Winans, it's so nice to see you again."

"How is he doing?"

I couldn't take my eyes off of his clothes as he was explaining how the operation went. I kept looking at him, watching him talk, but it was like I wasn't there. I couldn't focus on anything except the blood. It was then I realized it was Jeff's blood all over his clothes. I just kept staring at it. Oh my God, That's my husband's blood. I started to visualize the operating room and him cutting off his leg. I wondered what they did with his leg. Do they just throw it in the trash for the garbage men to pick up? As tears swelled up in my eyes, I drew myself back to his face. He was still talking and I hadn't heard a word he said.

"Mrs. Winans, do you have any questions? Mrs. Winans?"

Still in shock I said, "So, the surgery was a success?"

"He did very well". He lost a lot of blood, but he should be fine. Once the swelling goes down we will be able to fit him for a new prosthetic. Until that time, he will be on crutches. He should be able to go home in a week or so. I'll be doing a follow-up in 3 weeks at my office, so please call and set up his appointment. In the meantime, feel free to call me for anything."

"Thank you Doctor Brandies. I have to go pick up our son at school now. And I'll be back later. Please tell him I love him and I'll be back in a few hours."

I stood up, shook his hand, walked to my car and calmly drove off. As I was going across the Sunshine Skyway, I could still visualize

Dr. Brandies with Jeff's blood all over him. What was he thinking coming in to talk to me with Jeff's blood all over him? Jeff's blood. Jeff's blood! It kept escalating in my head.

I pulled off the road onto the embankment by the water, tears rolling down my face... Then it hit me. I couldn't let Travis see me like this. I looked around in the car for something to wipe my face with. I had to be strong for him. He's just a little boy and he's already been through so much.

I wiped my face with some left-over fast food napkins and thought, with my sunglasses on, Travis wouldn't know I had been crying. As I pulled into the school parking lot, I saw him come down the stairs from chapel. He was so beautiful, so innocent.

As he got in the car I asked "Hi "T" how was your day?"

"Fine, Mom. How's Dad?"

"I just left the hospital and Dad is doing great. In a few weeks he's gonna have a new leg, and it will work better than the one that was hurt. But, T, until they make a new leg, he's gonna need our help."

"I know, Mom. Then he smiled, "No problem."

"How about an ice-cream on the way home, and then we'll draw Dad a get-well card that I can take back to the hospital?"

"Okay, I know what I'm gonna draw for him and I can't wait for Dad to see it."

"He's going to be so excited that you were so thoughtful".

A week later, Jeff was home from the hospital and two months later he was fitted for a new prosthetic.

I was trying to figure out how I was going to pay the mortgage and put food on the table. We couldn't file bankruptcy anymore because we had to stay solvent for seven years. After selling the salon equipment, the only asset we had left was our Volvo station wagon. I knew what I had to do.

I found a pawn broker (loan shark) in Tampa who loaned me $1,500 on a Volvo that was worth $10,000. I was desperate, so I took it. I had 45 days to get the money, plus interest, or we would loose the car. On my way home it hit me like a lead balloon. What the hell had I just done? I had to let it go. One good sale would take care of everything.

I started praying for a buyer; just one. I started doing open houses for other agents in our office every weekend. I was running out of time. The third weekend after I pawned the car, I picked up a qualified buyer from an open house. They had their house under contract up north and it was supposed to close in two weeks. I found them a house in north St. Pete.

They decided to put an offer in. I was scared to death because I had only done "dummy" contracts in class. I thought Chris or someone would be in the office to help me, but when I arrived, no one was there. I went into panic mode, but then my sixth sense kicked in.

"Brandi calm down, it's gonna be all right. Just do the best you can."

I grabbed the paperwork out of the drawer, filled it out with the buyers, hoping I had everything. I called the listing agent and told him I had an offer on one of his properties and we set a time to meet at the seller's home. I was a nervous wreck. All the confidence I had an hour ago was falling by the wayside. Don, the listing agent, could tell in an instant, but he never said a word. He was a gentleman all the way.

Don asked that I step outside while he and his sellers talked things over. It was a good offer and a cash sale if my buyers deal went thru up north. A few minutes seemed like hours and then Don came outside.

"Brandi, come on in. It's a great offer. You did a great job presenting, but my sellers are countering with a different price."

I froze. I didn't have a clue about how to handle a counter offer. I looked at Don, and he could tell that I didn't have a clue.

"Don, this is my first offer and I will need your help to do a counter."

"I know," he said, comforting me. He took my hand and smiled. I started to quiver. "I'll make the changes and walk you through it."

"Thank you so much. You are my guardian angel tonight."

We got the changes done and the buyers accepted the counter price.

The next few weeks were hell. We had to have the home inspection, termite inspection, and all the other details. I was running out of time. I prayed everyday that we were going to have the closing on time.

I hadn't gotten my nerve up to tell Jeff what I had done, pawning our Volvo, but I would have to tell him soon enough.

Three days before I was going to lose our Volvo, the house closed. I walked into the pawn shop and handed the owner eighteen $100 dollar bills. I was hoping that this was a sign that things were going to turn around.

Chapter 18

A New Foundation

Three years had flown by since the move back to St. Petersburg. Jeff and I decided it was time to try and find an attorney in the Tampa Bay area who would take our case and help us fight for better NFL benefits.

Since the Hooper incident, and after trying to hire other attorneys in California, our luck with attorneys had not been very encouraging. One attorney we hired to finally get Jeff's Super Bowl ring, also took on Jeff's worker's comp case, but no one would take on the NFL. We had similar disappointments with another local attorney we hired in St. Petersburg. One thing I was learning about keeping my faith was that God's timing was not always our timing.

Occasionally doctors and nurses would ask Jeff to speak with other patients who were either terminally ill or severely injured. At first he said no, but when he did speak to the patients and families, it made him realize how fortunate he was in comparison. He often said that if he ever got surgery-free, he would like to start a foundation to help others.

A year after the BK, Jeff decided to go forward and start our non-profit foundation. He came up with the name Day for Our Children and the slogan, "Let's make everyday a day for our children." We weren't sure how to raise money, but Jeff knew how to play golf, so he decided we would go after local Celebrities and Corporations and put on celebrity golf tournaments with sports memorabilia auctions.

One thing that carried over from his football days was that when he wanted something, he was determined to persevere. I hadn't seen that side of Jeff for a long time. I was so proud of him.

He had some NFL alumni contacts and met with the Tampa Bay Bucs, Lightning, Orlando Magic and Tampa Bay Storm. It looked like this would be something that would give him focus on something other than himself. It was a constant struggle, with all the medication he had to take for headaches and other football injuries. He was trying to stay off of the pain meds during the day so he could function outside of the house.

He also met with Outback Steakhouse and GTE Mobil, based in Tampa, and presented sponsorship proposals to them. Then he contacted friends we knew from Alcoa Aluminum.

He was disappointed that he didn't get Outback or GTE as sponsors right away, but they were impressed with what he was doing. It was a good thing, because our first celebrity event was a total disaster yet a great learning experience.

We rented Al Lang Baseball Field in downtown St. Petersburg. Jeff arranged for the Celebs to play the Cardinals, rotating Cardinal's and Celebs on each team to make it fair. The morning of the event was gorgeous. Box office sales were great. By early afternoon, the weather took a very bad turn for the worse. Monsoon rains began about two hours before the game.

Our Celebs from Tampa and the surrounding areas were calling left and right cancelling. The little prima donnas would not play in the rain. To keep crowd control, we had enough players from the Cardinals and a few Celebs that showed up from the Pinellas side to play a six-inning game. It was hysterical to watch. The field was a huge mud puddle and everyone out there was slipping and sliding, but we pulled it off and saved face.

I think we lost about $2,000 by the time we paid for everything including the after party. The Celebs that did come out were the real heroes. They continued to help us for the next ten years as we put on events to raise money for our foundation and other charities.

The following year, we had our first celebrity golf tournament and sports memorabilia auction. Outback Steakhouse, GTE Wireless and Continental Airlines came onboard along with ASI Building Products. They became our key sponsors for ten years. Soon we started to get referrals from the local media.

Jeff also befriended Krawford Kerr, another former NFL Player. Krawford opened a number of restaurants in the Tampa Bay area called Winghouse.

Jeff always wore his Super Bowl ring when he went on appointments, and he had it on when he went to see Krawford one day about an upcoming event.

The Super Bowl ring was always a great conversation piece. Most people have never seen one up close. I was very privileged because I was one of the few wives that had a Super Bowl necklace. Champion teams could have the top part of the Super Bowl ring made into a necklace if they paid for it. It is something I treasure to this day.

Several times over the years, the top part of his ring came loose, and Jeff had it fixed and soldered. One side of the ring is customized with his name, helmet, and player number and the other side has the Super Bowl trophy, the names of the teams and the score. The top part had a total of three carats in diamonds, two one-carat diamonds and thirteen small diamonds in the image of a football. You cannot heat the white gold to a high temperature because it would melt and destroy all the custom work. The ring cannot be resized for that same reason.

A few minutes after Jeff came home from Krawford's, he came storming out of our bedroom with a look of desperation on his face. I knew something was terribly wrong.

He had his ring in his hand and said, "The football, with all the diamonds is gone".

Knowing what we had gone through to get it, I knew this wasn't something that could easily be replaced. We both went into panic mode and started tracking everywhere he had been. He also smoked at that time and had his hand out of the window most of the way home from the Winghouse. Searching twenty miles of highway would be an impossibility.

We searched the yard and the sidewalks where he had walked our dog. We went back to Krawford's place, then the dealership where

Jeff had gone to sign some papers on a car I was leasing. By the end of the afternoon, the Winans house was gloomy.

I decided that if we couldn't find the missing piece, I would give him the diamond football from my necklace for his ring. He seemed appreciative of that gesture.

He had to leave the next morning for an NFL physical in Miami. That morning, I took the trash can out to the road for pick-up. I checked the street and sidewalk area one last time–to no avail. Later that afternoon, after the trash had been picked up, I went to get it. As I wheeled it back up the driveway, I noticed something that seemed out of place.

I sat the can down, walked over, stooped down and picked it up. Why I did, I don't know, because it wasn't shiny until I turned it over. Low and behold, it was the missing diamond football! Somebody up there was looking out for us, and now I didn't have to sacrifice my necklace after all. When I told Jeff, he could not believe I had found it, and that it had been in the driveway all along.

One of the nurses Jeff met at All Children's Hospital through some of our charitable events would contact him when seriously and terminally ill kids needed a sports celeb boost. Jeff would be there in a heartbeat to help them out, even when he didn't feel up to it. It was good for him and it gave him some importance and renewed self-worth.

Jeff called Coach Perkins, the Bucs Head Coach, told him what he was doing for the kids at All Children's Hospital, and asked him for some Buc hats to give to the kids. Perkins said, "Winans, what do you want, a hand-out?"

That made Jeff so mad that he came home, took hats from his personal collection, and took them down to the hospital for the kids. He had never asked anyone for a hand-out. He couldn't believe that Coach Perkins had treated him like that. After that, Jeff wanted nothing more to do with him.

When Coach Sam Wyche came aboard, things were totally different. He and Rich McKay came out with a lot of the current and former NFL players and really supported our cause. I was so proud of what Jeff was doing to help families in the community, because I knew we were making a difference.

Jeff became very close to former Bucs coach, Abe Gibron, after Abe's stroke. Up until Abe's death, the two of them were inseparable. Both of them were disabled. They fought like cats and dogs. Abe's speech was almost indecipherable, and Jeff had a hearing problem from all the antibiotics he had taken over the years–but they were somehow able to communicate and loved each other like father and son. Abe's wife Suzie and I were so glad they had each other. Then Abe's health took a turn for the worse and he was gone. It was then I realized how much Abe had meant to Jeff.

Shortly thereafter, Michael Reith, St. Pete Limb and Brace owner, asked Jeff to speak with some new amputees. It was very therapeutic and Jeff loved doing it, but that didn't help his on-going headaches, deteriorating discs, and over-all depression. His anger would seem to come out of nowhere and for no reason. One minute he would be on top of the world and the next minute everyone was out to get him. I knew he was in a lot of pain all the time, but he felt that I never understood that.

He would make comments like, "You don't live in this body Brandi. How many surgeries have you had?"

It seemed to always be about him and what he was going through. Did he ever look at what I was going through? He didn't understand the pain in my back and neck, and what I went through every day to support the family and be a wife and mother to Travis. It hurt, but I loved him and tried to understand.

Sometimes he would feel bad about the way he treated us. He would call and apologize or write me more beautiful letters telling me how sorry he was to put me through this and how much he loved me, and I would melt all over again.

Travis was always so forgiving of his father's behavior. He was a very sensitive kid and we couldn't have asked for a better son. I don't think he had any idea how much he inspired his Dad and me to keep going.

Chapter 19

Sparring Partners

My mother's health was starting to deteriorate rapidly. I was still trying to get her to move in with us, and when the "no-name" storm hit in 1992, after refusing to evacuate off of Treasure Island, Jeff went over and physically picked her up and brought her to our house. I thought this would convince her to come and move in with us, but her stubborn dogmatic approach to life–my way or the highway, prevailed, and she refused.

She didn't want to be a burden on anyone, but she was my mother. She would never be a burden–maybe a pain in the butt sometimes, but never a burden. After the storm passed, she insisted on going home. Steve would visit and stay with her when he was in town. She loved baseball and football, and we would cook Sunday dinner for her, watch the games and have family days at her place.

Then one morning, around five in the morning, I got a call from Steve. He had been with Mom for a few days. "Mom's had an accident and you need to come over to her house right away."

I jumped up, got dressed and drove like a crazy woman. When I pulled up into Mom's circular drive, Steve met me at the door. The sun was just starting to come up.

I looked at him, concerned. "What's going on? What's happened to Mom? Where is she?"

"Mom fell again and she's in her bedroom," he said with a very calm voice.

As I walked into the living room, I called her name and started down the hall. Steve followed me. When I walked into Mom's bedroom, I saw her lying on the bed. She didn't appear to be in any pain. I looked at her face and followed it down to her legs. The left leg looked okay. The right leg looked odd, and then I realized that her right foot was upside down. I knew immediately that she had broken either her foot, leg or her hip.

I looked at Steve. "How long as she been like this?"

"For about three hours."

"Three Hours?" I looked at him very puzzled. "Why didn't you call an ambulance?"

He just stood there, cracking his jaw. He put his head down and just stared at the floor. I could feel my blood starting to boil. He was high on crack. He had a problem in the past, but I thought he had gotten past it. Apparently, he just picked her up off the floor where she fell in the living room, carried her to her bed, laid her down and just left her there. It wasn't worth an argument. I could see that he felt badly enough already.

I called the ambulance and then walked into the master bedroom where Steve had gone. He was sitting on the bed, looked up at me like some little kid who was about to be scolded.

"After the ambulance leaves, you're going to the hospital with me. When we get Mom secure, you're coming back here, packing your things and going back to your house. I'm calling a locksmith today and having the locks changed. If you want to do drugs, do them somewhere else. I won't let you drag us down. I have enough drug problems with Jeff at my own house.

"Do we understand each other? I love you Steve, but you need to get some help. Until you want to do that, I can't be around you, and neither can Travis. I don't understand why you want to self-destruct. You can tell your girlfriend if she wants to see you, she knows where you live."

Steve had recently found out he had a son twenty-four years old by an old fiancée he was engaged to in his early twenties. She never told him she was pregnant, but decided to contact him because she had a severe asthma attack and had almost died.

Whenever Steve was overly stressed, he turned to drugs. I just couldn't handle his problem right now. I had to concentrate on my mother.

We got Mom to the hospital. When they learned what had happened, the paramedics yelled at Steve for moving her and explained that he may have done more damage.

The doctor came out after the x-rays and said that Mom broke her hip. The hip had broken off at the main joint connecting it to the leg. The surgery went well and she would start rehab in a few weeks.

I let my other brother George know what happened. It was a long recovery for Mom. When she was finally back home at her house, she insisted on staying there.

She was driving me crazy and I was very frustrated. She refused to take any pain medication and was back on the beer. It was comical to see her pushing her walker to and from the bathroom trying to hold on to a can of beer. At least she was getting her exercise. I had to let it go. I hired a girlfriend from the salon to come over from four to eight four days a week. Donna would prepare Mom's meals; clean the house and they would sit watch the six o'clock news and chat about everything.

Every Sunday, Jeff, Travis & I would go over to Mom's house, go swimming and watch football or baseball. She was always so excited to see Travis. Sometimes Steve and Barbara (Steve's old fiancée) and Alton, Mom's new-found other grandson, would join us.

Alton finally found out that Steve was his father. He had a hard time accepting all of it and was somewhat overwhelmed. He needed a place to stay and was now living with us while he and his father were trying to get to know each other.

I had so much on my plate. I was working full time. Travis was in school, Alton was working, so Jeff was home alone a lot and started to feel left out. He would get mad at me anytime I was doing something with anyone else. At times he even seemed jealous of Travis. He resented Alton staying with us because Alton was Steve's son and he and Travis shared bunk beds in Travis's room. Eventually Alton moved back to Jacksonville.

He didn't want me to see Steve, who had gone into rehab at the VA. Jeff and Steve had a love/hate relationship. Steve didn't like the way Jeff was treating me. I needed an outlet.

My girlfriend Petie and I talked about getting into another exercise program.

One day we were at the Ringside Café in St. Petersburg having lunch. "I know what we could do."

I thought, "Here we go."

"We can start boxing. We're in pretty good shape."

Joking around, I said, "Yeah, we can go take some lessons. By the way where are we going to do that?"

"Smart ass," she said in a serious tone, "next door at the Fourth Street Boxing Gym."

"Right," I laughed, "with all the other boxers. Ha. Anyway, I don't think it's a co-ed boxing gym."

"Well, let's check it out after lunch."

"All right."

I was thinking to myself that we would go in and she would realize that it wasn't for girls. Then we could leave and continue our other workouts together somewhere else.

So after lunch we walked over to the Boxing Gym. The outside looked like a Marine Corp. hutch we lived in one summer while my Dad was in the Marines. The hanger doors were open and there were two men standing behind the counter as we walked in. The gym was what I would call a typical "spit" gym.

I had hung out with several boxers, when I lived in Santa Monica, through some other friends. Through them I met the Quarry brothers, George Foreman and Ken Norton. Once in a while we would fly to Vegas for a Main Event.

Looking around the gym, I noticed fresh blood on the floor of the ring. The decorations were not anything to write home about either: tall mirrors on the walls, three heavy bags, two speed bags, some exercise equipment and a big red bell. No air conditioning and no heat. I wasn't sure when the last time the place had been cleaned, but I knew it had been a while.

One of the guys behind the counter said "Hi, can I help you?

Petie said, "Yes, we want to learn how to box and we were wondering if anyone gives lessons."

I looked at her and said, "Lessons?" as I rolled my eyes.

Another man behind the counter had a big smile on his face and started shaking his head as if we were crazy.

The man who had asked if he could help us said, "Hi, I'm Guy, I'm one of the trainers here and I would be happy to work with you."

"Are there any other women who come in here and work out," I asked

"Yes, we have two other women who come in." Then he looked over at the other man, "This is Rich. He's one of the owners. We train a lot of upcoming boxers out of this gym."

Petie looked at me, "Well?"

I looked at her, at Guy and Rich, and asked, "Why not. What do we need to do to sign up, and when do we start?"

Guy asked, "How about tomorrow morning at nine? Do you ladies want to spar in the ring?"

We looked at each other and smiled, "No, just exercise.

"We'll see," Guy said. "If you're still here in a few weeks, you'll want to spar."

I thought, yea, right. We just want to exercise. When I got home, I told Jeff what we had done. He started to laugh and then shook his head.

"How long will this last and how much is it going to cost?"

"We pay on a month-to-month, so if we find it isn't for us, we can stop anytime. Is that okay?"

"Fine," he said, still shaking his head.

Travis thought that it was really cool. He had trained in karate for a couple of years when he was five to seven years old. He was the youngest in his class to get a belt and was a natural athlete like his Dad. Jeff never considered me an athlete. I was a "girl."

The next morning, Petie and I got to the gym promptly at nine. Guy was the only one there.

He smiled, "Well ladies are you ready to learn how to box?"

He took us through what would be our normal routine. First, he taught us how to wrap our hands, shadow box and do a basic warm-up. By that time, we were ready to get the gloves on and hit the heavy bag. As I put my hands in the gloves, I could feel the cold sweat left over from some the night before. Yuk! Okay, maybe I was a girl.

Once I got past that, (I ordered my own gloves) it felt good to hit something that was legal. Up until then I hadn't realized how much frustration had built up in me from the emotional weight I had been carrying around. Once I started, I couldn't stop hitting the heavy bag, grunting and groaning, until Guy walked over and tapped me on the shoulder.

"You might want to save some of that for the speed bag."

We had a great work out; we were exhausted–and we were hooked.

I called Petie the next day. "Girl, tell me that you are hurting from that work out yesterday."

She was. Neither one of us could walk or raise our arms or bend our thighs. But by Monday, we were ready to go again. Within three weeks, we were in the ring sparring and doing stronger workouts in the ring with the mitts. It was the best thing I had ever done for my PMS and stress.

Jeff thought boxing would be a short-lived adventure, until he realized how much I loved it. He began to get jealous of Petie and the time I was spending at the gym. He always had an open invitation, but he chose not to come.

The workouts seemed to help the pain in my neck and back. I also noticed that being around other people made me realize just how dysfunctional our household had become.

Travis started little league practice, and in October of 1993, Jeff's parents came for a surprise visit in their motor home. It was the first time they had come for a visit since we had moved, back in 1988. They had driven to Branson, Missouri–which isn't anywhere near St. Pete, Florida–and decided at the last minute to come for a visit. It was great to see them and it was good for Jeff, too. He needed them. I don't think they realized how much.

Travis was always excited to see them, as they traveled a lot. We talked them into staying a few extra days, so they could see Travis play Little League baseball. Travis was a catcher and was pretty good. They seemed to enjoy watching him play and I was glad they stayed.

I respected them because they were Jeff's parents, and I love them very much. But no matter how hard I tried, they never seemed to quite let me in. I felt like Ben Stiller in the movie Meet the Parents when his girlfriend's father wouldn't let him in the "circle." Nevertheless, we had a nice visit and they left a few days later.

We got back into our daily routine of life. Over the last few years, Jeff and I had started drifting apart. Most of the time he lived in his own little world in one part of the house and Travis and I lived in the other.

Jeff's mood swings were becoming more and more irrational and his drug use was continuing to increase. Except for the foundation and Travis, we really didn't seem to have a lot in common anymore.

He had worked hard getting the foundation off the ground and I was very proud of him. Due to the amount of wish-granting requests we were getting, we decided to add a wish-granting organization to our resume. Through the celebrity events we put on we met some people who were involved with an organization called Give Kids the World.

After visiting the facility, we knew we wanted to get involved. Families came from all over the world with their terminally ill children, to spend a week of heaven in Orlando. Families had to be referred by a wish-granting organization. Our foundation, would screen the applicant and put up their $300 fee.

Other people and organizations started coming out of the woodwork to get involved or to become a charity to which we would donate funds.

Our first major celebrity golf tournament was at Pasadena Yacht and Country Club in St. Petersburg. Along with celebrities who were football (a number of Bucs), baseball and hockey players, our guest list included: Otto Graham, Peter Marshall, Sam Wyche, Rich McKay, Lee Roy Selmon, Frank Robertson, Paul Delgato, Abe Gibron, Dick Crippen (our M.C.), and the local CBS television affiliate. A celebrity played in every foursome.

Outback Steakhouse provided food all along the golf course, it was the first time they had ever done that. GTE Wireless provided phones for the players on the course. These were all Jeff's ideas. Through his contacts we were able to provide autographed sports memorabilia for the silent and live auctions.

Our first tournament raised money for The Children's Home in Tampa. Eventually, we showed them how to do their own tournaments. It was first class all the way. We had Moon Bay Carved Glass do a tribute to Abe, and his son Kal presented it to him. It was a huge success and it looked like we had found our niche.

With football in season, Jeff spent a lot of time at the Bucs camp, now that Perkins was gone and Sam Wyche was there. The old equipment manager, Frankie Pupello, had stayed on and helped us get autographed items for our auctions.

During the success of the foundation, however, Jeff's headaches became worse. The numbness in his arms and the pain in his neck also worsened, as did his problems sleeping. Throughout our marriage, I don't think we actually went to bed together more than a dozen or so times. I had to get up early, get Travis off to school and go to work. Jeff would go to bed around two or three in the morning and sleep until ten or eleven.

Dr. Clarke, a local neurosurgeon, sent him to get another MRI. It revealed that he had a bone pressing on his spinal cord. This required a very serious and delicate operation to correct. They had to go in the front of the throat, move the vocal box over and remove the bone.

At first, the operation was a success; the numbness in his arms was gone and the headaches subsided. But as time went on, the severe headaches returned and the physical disabilities from his back, knees and ankle continued to deteriorate. Once again, I was juggling work, hospital, son, and taking care of my mother. Some days it was almost more than I could handle.

Then, without warning, her health took a turn for the worse. I begged her, once again, to come and live with us. She refused because didn't want to be a burden. I couldn't convince her otherwise. After several emergency visits to the hospital, she finally agreed to go into a nursing home where she could get the kind of care she needed.

I was very discouraged with the facilities I looked at. I wouldn't have put my worse enemy in some of these places–they were so dirty and depressing. My family doctor recommended that I take a look a Catholic nursing home called Maria Manor. It was about fifteen minutes from our house. As soon as I walked through the door, I knew Mom would love it. The energy was high. The living room was very homey, with a baby grand for the piano player who came and played in the afternoons. There was a gift shop and a beauty salon. If Mom improved, they had assisted living apartments. From her years of smoking, she had also developed emphysema and was now on oxygen.

We were able to move her into a private room near the nurse's station on the second floor. Jeff took in autographed photos for everyone. We always had a bowl of candy in her room, so she constantly had staff coming in and talking to her.

I was able to see her a lot because she was so close to the house. Every Friday afternoon, I would wheel her downstairs on the elevator so she could get her hair done. Her move to Maria Manor took a lot of stress off all of us. I didn't worry about her, knowing that if something happened, someone was there. She liked all the attention she was getting. Best of all, without the alcohol consumption, I started seeing my old Mom. It was heaven, and we became closer than we had been in years.

Travis was allowed to visit, she always lit up when he came in. I was disappointed that Steve had not come to visit her. The only thing he seemed to have time for was the crack cocaine. I didn't understand why, but I continued to pray for him every day. I knew it was an illness as well as an addiction. He was also diagnosed with bipolar, manic depression, and suffered from PTSD from Vietnam.

A few months after Mom was in to the nursing home, a nurse called to say that she was having abdominal pains and was on her way to the hospital. She hadn't been feeling well earlier that day and she was getting worse.

"We don't want to take any chances," the nurse said.

"Thank you. I'm on my way."

By the time I got there, Mom was in emergency surgery for a bowel obstruction. The operation was successful, but during her recovery, she developed pneumonia.

We were supposed to go to Jeff's parents for Christmas. I told Jeff to take Travis because I was going to stay here with Mom. He said he wasn't going if I didn't go. He was very understanding. I went to see Mom the next morning. She was weak.

"Mom, we're not going to California for Christmas."

"Please go, Brandi."

"No Mom, if something happened to you while I was gone, I could never forgive myself."

She looked at me with a serious expression. "Well if I die while you're gone, they can just put me on ice until you get back."

I looked at her surprised, and then we both started laughing. "Mom, I'm not going anywhere. End of conversation."

"Okay," she replied softly. She still had her sense of humor.

Steve's drug problem had escalated into a non-stop problem. I was begging him to get some help. Crack was the most evil thing I had ever seen. People's lives were destroyed just as Steve's was being destroyed. I had to turn it over to God. I was already too emotionally involved and I realized that his destiny, like all of ours, is in God's hands.

On December 23, 1993, Jeff and I came by after dinner to see Mom at the hospital. I had been sick with bronchitis and hadn't been able to see her for a few days. The nurses caught me in the hallway as we were going in her room.

"Mrs. Winans, can we have a minute with you please?"

"Of course," I replied.

"Your Mom is not doing well. It will be only a matter of hours before she passes. We have her on code, and we'll do our best to revive her if necessary."

I looked at the nurse. "She doesn't want to be on code. She wants to go in peace. Check her records."

"Well the doctor has her on code and we can only take her off if the doctor takes her off. You'll have to call the doctor."

"Can you get him on the phone for me? I'm going in to see my Mom right now."

When we walked into her room, she was sitting up in bed gasping for air. She was completely awake, smiling at us and appeared to be in no pain. It was obvious through her gasps for air that she couldn't talk, so I just smiled back at her and waved. It was difficult for Jeff to see Mom this way. All of his family members were still alive. I could see that he had never experienced this kind of loss. He was puzzled at my reaction.

"I love you, Mom," I said.

She looked at us so lovingly. "I love you, too. Now if you'll excuse me, I'm going to see your father."

Tears swelled up in my eyes. I blew a kiss at her. Jeff smiled at her and we walked out of her room. I knew it would be the last time we would see her alive. I went to the nurse's station. Her doctor had not called back, so I told her to have him call me at home.

The silence was deafening on the way to the car. There were no words that could be spoken at a time like this.

"I need to run by and tell Steve."

Jeff's whole demeanor changed. "Why, he hasn't even seen her in three months!"

He was angry at Steve for not coming to visit or call. I saw how much Jeff loved my Mom. Before she moved in the nursing home, he would go over to visit and help her run errands, and with the yard when he was able.

"That's why, honey, if I don't go by and let him know that she's dying and he should go see her, I could never live with myself."

Steve wasn't home, so I left a note on his door.

About half an hour after we got home, Mom's doctor called. I told him that he needed to check her records because she didn't want to be on code. It was a very emotional phone call. I selfishly wanted her to be around so she could watch and share her grandson grow up, but I knew I had to respect her wishes—something my father had been denied when he passed away. Then I realized that spiritually, they were always around.

Just after midnight I got a call from the head nurse. "Mrs. Winans, there's not much time; you need to come to the hospital."

Normally I would have jumped up and rushed out the door. I knew what was coming. Instead, I was calm and felt an enormous amount of peace. I got up and made a small pot of coffee.

As I got dressed, something strange and wonderful happened. I felt Mom's presence all around. I got goose bumps. She was there in the bedroom with me. I wasn't afraid. I started saying out loud, in a whisper, "Fly Mom. Don't stop, keep going, keep going, don't stop, don't stop, keep flying Mom, keep flying," and then she was gone.

I drank my coffee and got to the hospital around one in the morning. As I got off the elevator, the nurses were waiting for me.

"She's already gone, isn't she?"

"Yes, she's already gone. How did you know?"

"Because her spirit was all around me forty five minutes ago." They looked at me as if I was crazy.

I went into her room and sat down next to her bed and stroked her hair. She was so peaceful. I knew she was with my Dad. It was December 24th 1993, the day before Christmas.

I told Jeff what had happened when I got home. He was there for me; we just cried and hugged each other. I really needed that from him. I was so exhausted. A few minutes after my head it the pillow, the phone rang.

It was the Treasure Island Police. "Mrs. Winans, we have your brother Steve here. He was caught breaking in through a window at a house on Island Drive. He says he owns half the house with you.

"You have my brother? He broke into our Mother's house?" I couldn't believe it. "Sir, he used to own half of my mother's house but I've cashed him out."

"Can you come down to the station and bring that paperwork?"

"No sir, I cannot. Our mother died a few hours ago. I'll be happy to bring the paperwork down tomorrow, but not tonight. I'm not going to press charges against my brother, but can you hold him there and release him in the morning?"

"Yes Ma'am, I can do that. I'm sorry about your mother."

"Thank you," I replied. "Will you please tell Steve that our mother died tonight?"

"Yes, I will tell him".

"Thank You."

I hung up the phone and thought, "Perfect timing Steve, perfect timing."

The next morning was harder than I thought it would be. I had never taken care of anyone's funeral arrangements. Mom bought her plot years before right after Dad died. She had lost so much weight; I had to buy her a new suit. That was hard, she was a perfectionist. Everything seemed to be in a fog, but when I found the perfect suit, it was as if Mom was there directing me–with all of the accessories. After Dad died she became a fashion coordinator at a local department store.

That night, Christmas Eve, our family tradition was to open up one present. Earlier in the day I told Travis that Ma Ma Marge had gone to be with Jesus and Papa George.

"Okay, T, which present do you want to open tonight?"

With a big smile he said, "I want to open up one of Ma Ma Marge's presents"

He was so cute. He loved Mom so much and, of course, she spoiled him rotten. He picked one from underneath the tree. He knew every present that was for him.

After he opened up the present, a game for his Game Boy, he looked up at the ceiling and said, "Thank you, Ma Ma Marge. Thank you. I hope you have a good Christmas with Jesus."

My eyes swelled up with tears.

He looked over at me, "Mom, what's wrong?"

"Nothing honey, that was so beautiful. I'm glad you liked her present. I love you."

"I love you, too, Mom. Let's see what Ma Ma Marge got you."

It was priceless. Jeff was really moved and pretty silent that evening. We all mourn in our own way.

On my way back from the funeral home the next morning, I saw Steve walking on the sidewalk toward my house. I stopped and put the window down. "Need a lift?"

He opened up the door and got in. He looked awful. Breathing hard, he broke down and started to cry. We pulled into the driveway, and I went around to his side of the car, held out my arms, and we embraced each other.

"I need to get some help Brandi," he said sobbing. "I'm sorry I broke into Mom's house."

"I know you're sorry, but you need to get some help. I'll do whatever it takes to help you get some as long as you mean it."

I had him scheduled a few weeks before at the VA and he didn't show up for the appointment.

"Let me call Bob and see what we can do. I have to go back to the funeral home later and pick out a casket. Do you want to come with me?"

"No, there's no way I could handle that right now. I'm going home, take a shower and try and get some rest. Please help me to get some help Brandi, please!"

Because of the Christmas holiday, we buried our Mom the following week. She had become a recluse for the last three years. It was nice to see some of hers' and Dad's old friends.

After the funeral, a group of us went to the Sirata Beach Resort and had a few drinks in Mom's honor. Steve reiterated his plan to seek some help. It seemed like her death was the breakthrough he needed.

The VA wouldn't let him in right away, because he had stiffed them before, so I talked to Jeff about helping him until Mom's house sold. I contacted Charter Hospital in Tampa and he agreed to go. Jeff and I fronted the $12,000 they required up front. Five days later, he checked himself out. He told me that since he wasn't going through withdrawals, they told him he could go on their outpatient program. He lied. You can lead a horse to water, but you can't make him drink. Disappointment set in, and I had to let it go. All I could do was pray there would be another day when he would have the strength to mean it.

Chapter 20

Unfair Competition

Within a few months, the close ties Jeff and I felt after Mom died soon started to fade away. We were back in our routines again. My real estate career was taking off. I had made Senior Associate and specialized in corporate re-location. Still, I needed something more.

I signed on with a local talent agency and started getting some work as an actor. Once Travis found out, he wanted to act too. He was a natural and signed on with their children's division. We started spending more time together going on auditions. Jeff was having a hard time dealing with it.

At times, we had to walk around as if we were on eggshells. Laughing too loud and having fun meant we must be up to something and his verbal abuse was becoming constant. I don't think he realized how much he was pushing us away

Every time I felt like I couldn't take anymore, he would apologize in a letter or do something sweet and romantic and I would melt. But in between those times, I was starved for attention. I tried not to let it get to me, because I felt a lot of it stemmed from all the drugs he was taking. He didn't want me around. When I wasn't around, he wanted me at home. It was very confusing and hard for me to keep confidence in myself when I was at home. Outside of home, I knew who I was and I liked myself.

Sometimes I felt he used his disabilities as a crutch, or as an excuse to get what he wanted. It was important for me to try and keep things as normal as they could be for Travis, but kids see everything. They're like video recorders with legs.

Petie and I continued to box and it was something I looked forward to. We worked out three times a week and befriended the other female boxers. Sometimes a group of us would box or go out together. That way, I could release all the frustrations I felt at home.

One day, out of the blue, Guy, our trainer at the gym, took me totally off guard and told me that he was in love with me, and said he wanted me to divorce Jeff and marry him.

So boxing at the gym, my only outlet, ended that day. With my marriage already so fragile and Jeff's emotions running so deep, I made an appointment to see a Christian marriage counselor who my girlfriend recommended. I asked Jeff to go with me.

The day before the counseling session, it came out about what Guy had said to me. Jeff exploded, and by the time we got to the counselors office, he had come to his own conclusions. In his eyes, I was some low-life cheating wife. There was nothing I could do to convince him otherwise. A few days after we went to the marriage counselor, I suddenly had two men fighting over me. I became very confused.

"Brandi, I realize how much I've hurt you and not been there for you. I do love you and I don't want to lose you," Jeff pleaded.

It had been so long since I had heard him say those words. I just felt like the only reason I was there was to be the caretaker, the housekeeper and the nanny.

"I have a lot to think about. I'm glad you told me how you feel. There's a lot more at stake here than just us. We have to think about Travis."

It would have been easier to compete with another woman than compete with his drugs. I often wondered if he wasn't seeing some as well. I didn't want our marriage to end, but I wanted to feel needed and loved. As a friend, Guy made me feel special. I questioned our friendship. Had it become more?

The counselor suggested that we take some time away from each other. Earlier, we had planned a trip to North Carolina. He said there was no way that Jeff and I should go together, so Travis and I ended up going alone. I had time to do a lot of thinking about Jeff and me and made some strong-willed decisions that week.

I called Jeff from North Carolina. "If you meant what you said, I'd like to try and see if we can save our marriage. But I can't live the way I have been living and Travis and I can't compete with your drugs. Maybe we could try some more marriage counseling. What do you think?"

"I know I have a lot of issues that I have to do deal with. I can quit the drugs on my own if I want to. I know you have to work, but I feel like you are never around. I get bored during the day. I have a lot of pain. Maybe more marriage counseling might help. I'm willing to give it a try. We've had fourteen years together."

"Maybe you should think about writing a book about everything we've been through? It would occupy your time and you wouldn't be so bored."

"I'll think about it."

I couldn't wait to get home. Jeff was waiting for us in the driveway when we pulled up. He opened the door, pulled me into his arms and gave me one of the most passionate kisses I had ever received. Travis was in awe. Then we got the typical kid's expression of "Yuk." Jeff walked around the car, gave Travis a big hug and helped us carry in the suitcases.

For the next few months, our relationship was stronger than ever. Then, it all started to slip away. Marriage counseling wasn't working anymore, and without warning Jeff would sabotage everything we had built up and go off on these violent tangents about Guy. Then accuse me of being with other men. I would try to defend myself, but that only made things worse.

I took it over and over again until I stopped trying to explain myself. I knew who I was. I liked myself, and God knew who I was. That was all that mattered. I continued to pray every day that Jeff would find himself. Instead, he seemed to go deeper and deeper inside himself. Where it would all end?

Chapter 21

Contractor Nightmare

Mom's house had been up for sale for over a year and a half before it finally sold. Steve was in and out of rehab and was now over at the VA in Tampa for long-term treatment. The sale of her home was the last of my inheritance. Jeff insisted on using it to remodel the house. I was apprehensive, because we almost had the house paid off, but I knew there would be no peace until he got his way.

After getting three bids, we decided to go with a contractor referred by one of Jeff's best friends. He appeared very reputable, drove a new Beamer and often played in our celebrity golf tourneys.

Unfortunately, he turned into the contractor from hell. When mechanic's liens started arriving in the mail, and one of his workers told us we were nowhere near finished, we confronted the situation. He had been taking the draws, but wasn't paying the subcontractors. He had never done a remodel before. In fact, we found out later that he didn't even have a license or any insurance we could file a claim against.

I called the State Attorney's office and we filed criminal charges. We ended up paying the subs that hadn't been paid for what they had completed, and then pay other subs to finish the job. I thought we would recover the money. By the time it got to court, the contractor plead that he was broke. With him having no money to pay us back, the court ordered a settlement of $7,500. We got $200 per month payments until it was paid off.

Nine months later, the house was finished and we were broke. We were six months without a kitchen. With the income from my job and Jeff's small pension, we were barely making ends meet.

During all of this, Gene Upshaw fought and finally won a new union collective bargaining agreement. This allowed free agency, and an increase in Jeff's non-football related disability pension from $970 to $1,600 a month.

The extra income helped out a lot. With the real estate market down, I wasn't making a lot of money for the time I was putting into my job. Then my business partner decided to retire.

Travis was doing well in school and growing like a weed. He was living and breathing basketball. I couldn't get Jeff out of the house unless it was something he wanted to do. He would make most of his basketball games. He was so proud of Travis. Other than that, Travis and I were pretty much on our own.

I was beginning to wonder if there was another woman. He would pick fights and then storm out of the house. He would leave several times during the day to get a soda at the local convenience store and be gone for hours. I even hired a private detective, but an hour after I hired him; I called and asked for my money back. I decided I wasn't going to stoop that low.

I started worrying about myself for a change and made an appointment to see Jack, another counselor my girlfriend was seeing. A few weeks later, Jeff surprised me and decided to make an appointment with my counselor, too. I felt like he wanted to see if I was telling the truth. He questioned almost everything I did or said.

To my surprise he and Jack really hit it off. They would talk about everything. After a few individual sessions, Jack brought the two of us together. He gave each of us assignments. I was to talk more to Jeff about things going on with Travis and me, and Jeff wasn't to lie to me anymore about drugs or money. The last time he agreed to do that was when we were living in Turlock, when we met with the SSI counselor.

We seemed to be a team again. The change in him was amazing and his mood swings weren't as great. I assumed it was because we were in counseling. However, his headaches and disorientation continued–along with the deterioration of his physical injuries.

With the real estate market down, my girlfriend Petie and her husband John offered me a job at their print shop. I decided to leave real estate and give it a try. Over the next couple of years, I worked for the Maguire's as Director of Marketing and VP Operations Officer for Express Communications. Both were friends who needed my help. They didn't realize how much they were helping to keep us afloat.

Jeff decided to try and get out more, started going to go to a few meetings of the local NFL alumni chapter. He had a lot of the former players involved in our annual tournament and his participation was great PR for the tournament.

The foundation was something we had always done together and I had gotten more involved in it as Jeff's body deteriorated. His arms and fingers had tingling sensations and sometimes he had no feelings in them at all. He would drop things and then get mad at himself taking his frustrations out on Travis and me.

I would try and cover it up by saying, "Travis, Daddy is on his funny pills, so don't do anything that will get him upset."

Travis would say, "No, duh, Mom."

With another bone pressing on Jeff's spinal cord from all the hits he had taken as a lineman, more surgery was inevitable. This one seemed to help. Jeff's attitude improved, and like the roller coasters of life, our marriage seemed to be back on track.

Chapter 22

Another Chance

Travis was in middle school at St. Petersburg Christian School. He still lived and breathed basketball and was playing on a local city league. He also loved to draw in pencil and was an expert at any Nintendo games. Playing Nintendo with him made me feel like a fifth grader again.

Every year we would get two personalized benefit books from the NFL–a retired pension book and a supplemental disability book. Every year since 1981, Jeff was sent to see a NFL neutral physician for an annual physical to determine if he still qualified for disability benefits. They send you at your own expense and then reimburse you if you continue to be disabled. We never knew where they were going to send Jeff. This time they were sending him to see a doctor in Miami.

October 1996, the new disability and pension benefit books arrived and I saw that a new football-related disability category had been added called "degenerative disc football related." Total and permanent disability from football related injuries (which we felt we had always been entitled to) was now up to $ 12,000 per month. The football related degenerative disc category was $4,000 per month– a big difference from the $1,600 we were getting. Excited, I showed the book to Jeff.

"Honey look."

"I read it," he said sarcastically.

"Well, you need to write a letter asking to be re-classified."

"It's just a waste of time! They aren't going to change anything. Look how many years we've been fighting with them."

He never gave me any credit for getting us his NFL or the SSI disability, and somehow after we got it, it always became "his" money. It hurt. His personal allowance always came off the top of his monthly disability checks. I was supposed to use the rest of it, along with my income, to pay all the bills.

I decided to write the NFL on my own requesting that Jeff be re-classified to the new football related category of degenerative disc. I also asked for his re-classification to be retroactive and that we be allowed on the next board meeting docket.

The NFL response came a few weeks later, saying they would check into it and anything I wanted to say could be put in writing, and it would be read by each of the board members. I put together a formal letter and attached all of our records.

We were tabled at the first board meeting, stating that they had a new board and had added a seventh board member who was an NFL neutral physician. I felt that could be beneficial to us as he would know how to read and interpret the physician's reports.

Jeff was his pessimistic self with his, "I told you so," routine. After the next NFL board meeting, we got a letter stating that he was tabled again. This time they were sending him to see a different neutral physician in New Jersey, and wanted us to pay for the trip. We were told that if the physician deemed Jeff disabled they would reimburse us. I called and told them we were a hardship case, and since they requested that Jeff travel, they should have to pay for it. They agreed and booked the flight.

A few weeks later, he flew to New Jersey. Jeff said that when he walked into Dr. Tria's office, there were two other players there that he knew who were also being seen by Dr. Tria. He seemed to be very in tune with Jeff's injuries, doing a thorough physical and Jeff felt that it went well.

We were scheduled for the next board meeting. Jeff was tabled again. This time the board wanted him to see an NFL neurosurgeon. We scheduled that appointment in Atlanta.

I knew that the NFL board couldn't put us off anymore–or so I thought. Then, we got another letter from the board. Jeff was tabled again. This time they wanted a letter from Social Security Disability stating that Jeff was on disability and copies of our income tax returns for the last five years. They said that would provide proof that Jeff hadn't had any income from an outside job. Jeff was furious and again, "I told you so," came out of his mouth.

"It's just their way of justifying your new classification," I said.

Jeff took it personally, because ever since he left football, we were treated as if we were looking for a handout. The NFL had done everything they could not to pay Jeff anything. Even after we won our arbitration in 1984, they used the gunshot accident as another ploy to keep his pension low. It wasn't just about Jeff.

"Don't worry," I said, "I'll put the paperwork together. You call Social Security and get the summary the board wants and I'll get the copies of our tax returns together.

The Social Security paperwork didn't come in time. Somehow it got lost in the mail. I called and had us on the docket for the next board meeting, which wasn't going to happen for another four months, letting them know what happened with Social Security, and backed it up with a fax.

One thing I learned a long time ago was that you must verify and document everything. Jeff always wanted me to throw out all of our old paperwork because of the space it took to keep it. This time he was glad that I had saved it.

The paperwork arrived in Washington and we were finally put on the docket for October 1997. In November of 1997 we received a letter from the NFL stating that Jeff had been approved for re-classification to the degenerative disc category. For the first time in almost seventeen years, we wouldn't have to struggle to make ends meet. They only made it retroactive for the six months. After years of fighting, our persistence and fighting for what we believed in had finally paid off.

Jeff was still upset because they refused to give him full, total and permanent, football related disability, but this was a major breakthrough and victory. We sat side by side on our bed and re-read the letter over and over. The emotion was too much for me and I couldn't stop the tears. I knew that because of my persistence and millions of prayers, I had just secured our future.

"Brandi," Jeff said, "I don't want you working anymore. I can take care of you and Travis now. We don't have to struggle anymore." He put his arms around me and we just held each other.

I really thought that this would be the thing that would get Jeff to release all the prideful shame he had felt over the last sixteen years. He could hold his head high, but no amount of money could replace his emotional and physical deterioration.

Chapter 23

Another Remodeling

With our newfound income, Jeff decided to remodel the house again and build a second story. I was very apprehensive because of the last experience. I didn't really think we needed to add a second story, but he felt we could afford it and I knew how much he wanted it.

So, in 1998, we did another major renovation. We built an upstairs master suite overlooking the water and added the only "football" swimming pool in our area. The Pebble Tec finish added a realistic touch. We used white tiles for the shoelaces.

Jeff had always wanted a pool. We lived on the open bay, and the previous owners had built cement stairs going down to the small beach behind our house so we usually swam in the bay.

However, a few years before, right after we finished the first remodel, Jeff and Travis bought an above ground pool at K-Mart that costs about $400. Jeff had one of our workers dig the hole, level it out and he helped Jeff put it together. I had never seen anything like it before. It was really cute. I think it was about four feet deep. It even had a little chlorinator that floated on top of the water. It was funny to watch Jeff and Travis float around in their blown up rafts with their sunglasses on.

About three weeks after we got the pool, Jeff and I had a big fight. Travis was out for the night, and we were yelling at each other. It was storming outside and the winds were very high. I walked to the back of the house in the heat of our shouting match. As I looked out the back window, I realized that the pool was gone.

I did a double take and yelled back, "And your fricking pool is gone!"

"What?"

"Your fricking pool is gone, too."

"Yeah, right," he snapped back.

Jeff walked up behind me from the living room. There was nothing left of the pool except the bottom piece of the tarp. We looked at each other and started laughing. We forgot about the argument. I don't even remember what it was about. This pool was not going anywhere.

I took Jeff up on his offer and quit my job. I stayed active with Travis's school activities, the school booster club and helped Jeff with the foundation.

After seeing the transition that Travis went through as he entered adolescence, and how the schools were not offering any life skills–only academic core classes, I wrote a life skills program called The "Wanna be" Seminars (What do you want to be? How do you plan to get there?) Through that, I was able to get on the Pinellas County Schools Speakers Bureau. I found my niche.

In 1999, Travis started his freshman year of high school. He made the junior varsity basketball team while still playing on the local city league. He also did his last commercial for the Home Shopping Network channel.

Jeff wasn't having as many infections since the BK, but his neck, back and knee pain continued to get worse. He required more surgeries on his knee and back. Unfortunately, the knee surgery was not a success, and even seemed to make it worse. He changed doctors to Dr. Mike Smith and had the knee surgery done again. This one worked.

He had always claimed that when we got his disability money he would be happy. Then it was when we did the remodel, he would be happy. But each time after he got what he wanted, the happiness was short-lived and he would be looking for something else to make him happy. I didn't understand it. We had everything going for us, but it was never enough.

Over time, the drug use increased to where I couldn't take it anymore, and he couldn't take my badgering him about it anymore. We needed some time apart, so he decided to drive back to California and spend a few months out there.

In a desperate measure, I decided to call his family doctor. I wanted to know why he was dispensing so many prescriptions to Jeff, and how he was abusing them. The doctor admitted that he recognized the problem and wasn't going to prescribe any more meds for Jeff when he came back. Jeff was very persuasive and cunning when he wanted something. Celebrities and pro-athletes tend to get away with more. He said he would talk to Jeff and refer him to a local pain management clinic.

I felt guilty after I hung up, but Jeff needed help and I was afraid I'd come home one day and he'd be dead. I didn't want Travis to find his father like that.

I was noticing something else. We would have conversations and Jeff wouldn't remember them. At first, I thought he was just trying to pick a fight by accusing me of not having the conversations with him. Later it occurred to me, maybe, he really didn't remember.

He was only in California for three weeks before he came home. When he returned, he kept his appointment at the pain management clinic. In California, the pain management clinics teach patients how to manage pain without a lot of medication. I thought it would help him, but I found out very quickly that the pain management approach was different in Florida.

After a thorough evaluation, the clinic prescribed some very heavy medication, including Duragesic patches (80 times stronger than morphine, usually given to terminally ill cancer patient), Soma, Valium and Percodan. And because of his lower back pain, they scheduled him for him for surgical injections into his lower spine.

In 2000, after my begging him to get some psychological help and have some tests run, he made an appointment to see a forensic psychiatrist all on his own. His doctor diagnosed him with manic depression, bi-polar and borderline personality disorder. She prescribed Lithium and Wellbutrin XL to help his depression and mood swings.

I was so proud of him for finally going and prayed that maybe now he could find some peace within himself. Could he handle all of this medication? Or was the pattern going to repeat itself?

Chapter 24

My Brother's Legacy

Time was flying by. I rarely saw Petie anymore. One morning out of the blue she called and asked me to lunch. We got caught up on her daughters, Lacey and Riley, and my Travis. I forgot how much I missed her company.

Three weeks later, the early morning call from Petie was not a positive one. She was very upset.

"I'm sorry to call you so early. Are you up?"

"No."

"So you haven't you seen today's paper?"

"No. What's wrong?"

"I don't know how to tell you," she said as she started to cry. "Guy, our friend and former boxing trainer is dead."

"Dead, what are you talking about?"

"It's in the paper this morning. He was riding his bicycle and was hit a few days ago by a woman driving a van. He was taken to Bayfront Medical Center, and was in a coma for several days. The doctors said he was brain-dead and his father made the decision to pull the plug. His funeral will be in a few days and I wanted to see if we could go together."

"Thanks Petie, I appreciate that."

I had always wished the best for him. He was good man. He didn't deserve to die so young, but then we never know what God has in store for us. There were over 500 people at his funeral. He had made an impact on so many people's lives.

I started thinking about my Dad's death, My Mom's death, and my brother, Steve. Steve and I had been getting along for the last year and a half. He had gone through several more treatment programs, gotten married, and then became estranged from his wife. I helped him get an apartment on Madeira Beach that was within walking distance of everything. His mental illness and drug abuse had created convulsions, so he had lost his driver's license.

It was the first time we had spent any quality time together since we were teens. Unfortunately, a little over a year later, Steve's demons got the best of him again.

He decided to move to Lake City in a VA Retirement Community. He was doing really well there. The nurses and staff were wonderful and they really liked him. You could give him twenty minutes anywhere and he would know everyone and their life story.

July 26th, 2003, I got a call from one of the staff at the retirement community. Steve had asked for a five-thirty wake-up call, but he had died of a heart attack in his sleep. Massive guilt for not going to see him the last two months came rushing in. Jeff and Travis were supportive. Travis heard me on the phone talking to the nurse in Lake City. He walked into my office. I turned around, put my arms around him and he just held me while I cried. He and Steve had been very close before Steve got back into drugs.

I called Rich, one of Steve's best friends since junior high, to see if he would go up with me. Rich, Steve and four other friends joined the Army under the buddy system in 1965. Rich and his wife, Marie, were always there for Steve. I picked Rich up the next morning. It was a four-hour drive, so we had a lot of time to reminisce about old times.

Steve had lost almost everything over the years due to his drug abuse. When we walked into his tiny room, there was only his TV, his books, (he loved to read), the leather jacket in the closet, and a few other personal belongings. That was it. He was fifty-six years old. A few minutes later, a man knocked on Steve's door and came in. He smiled and said, "Are you Steve's sister?"

"Yes, I'm Brandi. This is one of Steve's oldest and dearest friends,

Rich."

"My name is John. Steve and I became good friends while he was here. Everyone here loved him. Your brother was one of the finest men I have ever known. He always made me feel worthy and to know that I had a purpose."

I gave him a hug. "Thank you so much for sharing your story."

As we were leaving, I went to the nurses' station to let her know who I was, and to thank her for taking care of my brother.

"Mrs. Winans, your brother took care of us. He was one of a kind."

As we were talking, an older lady with oxygen tubes in her nose and a walker with her oxygen tank attached came over." Are you Steve's sister?'

"Yes Ma'am, I am. This is one of Steve's oldest friends, Rich. He was one of the guys that Steve went into the service with to fight in Vietnam."

"If it wasn't for your brother, I wouldn't be here. He always gave me inspiration and hope."

One person after the next kept coming up to us telling a "Steve" story. It was so moving. Then it hit me. God had been using him to minister to all these hurting people. They never had any idea who he was. They only knew him as Sergeant Steve Grayson, a decorated Vietnam War hero who through his bravery with the First Calvary Division earned a Silver Star, a Bronze Star and two Air Medals. Steve was a crew chief on a helicopter. His unit was featured in the movie, We Were Soldiers.

The ironic part was they never knew that Steve was one of the best senior producer/directors and cameraman in the television news industry. He never boasted about himself that way. He was a commoner in their circles. That day, I understood that even through his demons, he was doing God's work. I was never more proud of him than I was that day.

Channel 13, did a beautiful tribute to him on the air and on their website. August, 2003, I had a wake for him at Gators on Treasure Island–thanks to Butch Ellsworth (another dear friend and Army buddy) and a lot of wonderful friends and family. I did a collage of photos and memorabilia he had collected over the years, and placed them on tables around the bar. Each one of us took the microphone and told a "Steve" story.

He was cremated and his ashes were scattered behind the hotel that our Dad managed, some at my house, and some in his crypt at the Florida National Cemetery in Bushnell, Florida. We never know when it's our time to go. That's what makes life is so precious.

Chapter 25

My Son's Turn

At first, the medications that Dr. Mayo had prescribed seemed to work. His mood swings diminished and we were getting along really well. Then almost overnight, his mood swings began to escalate. I felt like I was living with the Gestapo, and we were back at each other's throat.

During this time, Travis was caught in the middle. Without talking to Travis or me, Jeff started talking to some larger high schools and decided to pull him out of Canterbury. Canterbury was a small private high school where Travis started his freshman year and where a lot of his friends went. Jeff felt Travis could be seen more to advance in basketball.

One of Travis's friends, Sam, called him one night. "Travis, I hear you're going to St. Pete Catholic next year."

"No I'm not. Who told you that?"

"A kid I know who's on the basketball team."

Travis came out of his room and told us what Sam had said.

"Yes," Jeff said, "I've been talking to the other schools. It's for your own good and when I decide on what school will offer you the best deal, that's where you'll be going in the fall. I know what I'm doing."

Travis looked at his Dad and me in a way I had never seen him look at us before. It was a look of total betrayal, hurt and disappointment.

Then he did something he had never done before. He stood up

to his father and said firmly, "Dad, no I'm not. I love Canterbury. I know what you're saying, but I want to take this team where it's never gone before. You have to let me do that. Please, I can do it, Dad."

"Jeff, " I said, "listen to what he's saying, please. Don't do this in his last two years of high school. You can have him showcased to scouts. We can send out videos."

He looked at both of us and said disgustingly, "You two deserve each other. I can't believe that you're not backing me up on this, Brandi. I know what I'm doing and he's transferring!"

Travis walked back down the hall and slammed his bedroom door. I had never seen him so upset.

"Jeff, if you force him to go there, do you think he'll play basketball from his heart? If he doesn't play from his heart, he won't give it his all. You, of all people, should understand that. He'll resent you and nobody will win. This is his destiny, not yours. I know you see his talent and want the best for him."

"He's too young to know what he wants!" he shouted.

"Honey, he's been picking out his own clothes since he was three years old. If he fails at this, it will be his own doing. But have enough respect for him to let him try. He's set his own goals for the next two years. Give him a chance to show you."

He glared at me. "You have never played in the pros. You just don't get it! I'm done trying."

He turned around and went upstairs. I sat there for a few minutes and then went to check on Travis. He was sitting on his bed; tears were running down his face. He was so hurt that his Dad couldn't understand. He didn't want to disappoint him. He needed his Dad's acceptance more than ever. I could see in the end, he would give in.

At that point, I didn't know what to do. I just stood there. "Let's sleep on this tonight, T. Tomorrow is another day."

This isn't where I thought the family discussion would go. Siding with Travis only brought more friction between Jeff and me. My mistake was discussing it in front of Travis. I was sorry I did that, but I thought as a family we should discuss things openly so there was not any doubt what was being said. Jeff did not see it that way. Kids were meant to be seen and not heard. That's how he was raised.

A few days later, Jeff came up to me after breakfast. "I hope you're happy. Against my better judgment, I told Travis he could stay at Canterbury. I know in the end who'll be right, but we'll let you two see. Then you can be responsible for ruining his life, all right? I'll make arrangements with Lee at USF and some other schools to get him seen."

As the next few months went by, Jeff became more distraught over the decision he had made, and once again got more and more inside a bottle of pills. He would get his scripts filled for a thirty-day period and within two to two and a half weeks; he would go through all of them again. I realized what I thought was over, wasn't finished at all. Nothing had changed.

It wasn't healthy for Travis either. His Dad would pick on him constantly. He saw his Dad loaded a lot of the time. So did some of his close friends. I was making myself crazy, trying to protect every-one, knowing I couldn't.

Then, in his senior year of high school, Travis's basketball game exploded. He could do no wrong. As co-captain, he set his goals that year for the team and himself. His specialty was three pointers; he was the go-to guy. He scored 783 points and was the first kid at Can-terbury to make the 1,000 Point Club.

He was the leading scorer for Pinellas County for the whole 2002–2003 basketball season. It was one of the goals that he had set for himself that year and he accomplished it. He averaged 27.4 points per game with five games over 40 points and two games where he scored 49 and 50 points. He set records for Canterbury and took his team where they had never gone before. They had seven players on the team, then only six players for the second half of the season.

A local sports cable television station from Brighthouse came out and covered Travis and his teammates. They compared the team to the movie Hoosiers. With only six players and him being the go-to guy, Travis had to play every minute of every game. He had injuries and knee problems, but he was unstoppable.

He made All-State Honorable Mention by the Florida Writers As-sociation, All-County Honorable Mention, and played on the local All-Star team. It was an honor for him to be awarded Male Athlete of the Year. Jeff and I were so proud of him. Jeff and Travis seemed close again, and Jeff's expertise could help Travis with his game.

Jeff was right about one thing, the team didn't get the credit they deserved. They were a small private school, outranked by the larger schools. The scholarships that Travis deserved didn't come either. He was accepted at Florida Southern in Lakeland, Florida and started there in the fall of 2003, to go to school and play basketball.

I couldn't have been more proud of Travis than I was the day he graduated from high school in 2003. I was asked to be the MC for his senior dinner. We flew his grandparents out from California for his high school graduation.

It was the first time in our marriage (22 years) that they had ever stayed overnight with us. It was nice to see three generations all together and for Travis to be able to spend time with them as a family. A few months later, he was getting ready to fly out of the nest and off to college.

Jeff and I helped him pack. We followed him over to his college, with both cars packed. The dorms were so small. Travis was on staff at the exercise facility and they were to have training that week, so he arrived a week before his roommate, Troy, or any of the other students. Troy was another 6'8" player from Ft. Myers.

My Manx cat "Lightning" had died. My brother Steve had died unexpectedly, and now our only son was going off to college. That was a lot of emotion to take in two months. In between Steve's death and wake, we played "meet the parents" and invited Troy and his parents to come up for dinner at our home.

They were a very nice family. It's funny how you hope that whomever Travis would be rooming with has good study habits (maybe some of it would rub off on our son, ha) and be of good moral character (which Travis is). Troy seemed to fit at least with the good moral character. He and Travis were about the same on the scholastic side. We were relieved, and it was great to meet his parents.

The last of Travis's stuff was unloaded. Emotions were as thick and ignoring them was as impossible as trying to cut fog with a knife. Jeff hugged Travis and said he would wait for me at the car. I looked up at Travis and saw his bottom lip start to quiver. I smiled and took a deep breath. I stood on my tippy-toes and hugged him. I held him so tight. I thought, "God, please let me be strong when I look in his eyes."

"Well it looks like you have your work cut out for you, T, getting all of this stuff organized and setting up your computer. The good news is you get to pick your side of the room and learn about the campus and the fitness club before everyone else does."

He gave me that gorgeous smile.

"I love you," I said. "Remember, we're just a phone call away."

"I love you too, Mom."

I turned and walked out of his room, down the hall and out the front door of his dorm. Jeff was standing by the car smoking a cigarette. It was apparent that his emotions had overwhelmed him, too. Tears were evident in his eyes.

It was a long solemn ride home. It was the first time I had to "sever the umbilical cord." It wouldn't be the last.

I couldn't help but wonder where Jeff and I would go from here. It seemed like the main thing that had been keeping us together was Travis. Now Travis was gone.

Chapter 26

Faith Rekindled

With the loss of Steve, Travis at college, and Jeff and I bickering, I rekindled a friendship with my neighbor, Cay. God brought her back into my life at the time I needed her most, and she took me to a Joyce Meyer conference. It was then I realized how much my faith had dwindled. The thing that kept me going for years had been slowly slipping away.

For some reason, Jeff was very jealous of Cay. He felt threatened by her. Cay, like me, had a passion to help our youth. She loved what I was doing with the Wannabe Seminars. One day, she said, "Let's go to the juvenile detention centers and help the kids."

"How are we going to do that?" It's not that easy.

When God is ready to open doors, they open. She picked up the phone, got hold of the Assistant Superintendent and the next thing we knew, we were doing my Seminars and leading kids to the Lord. A year before, Juvenile Detention Centers in Florida and the Juvenile Justice Department had become faith-based.

I got re-signed on board the Pinellas County Schools Speakers Bureau for another year. I felt like a rookie Christian, sucking up and absorbing anything I could. I started journaling and listening to Him more when I asked for help. It wasn't a religious experience, it was a relationship. I was finding a kind of peace and joy that I never knew existed.

Travis was adjusting to college, but having trouble with his academics. He didn't realize there was so much reading in college and that there was no homework for extra credits. Reading was Travis's worst enemy. I knew how he felt. It was mine, too. I could get A's and B's in class and then flunk the exam.

His schedule was grueling. Up at five in the morning, in the gym at five thirty. Practice before classes, classes, working at the fitness club, more afternoon practices and tutoring at seven every night.

The basketball coach was a drill sergeant (which wasn't a bad thing) and he didn't/wouldn't let Travis do what he did best–shoot three pointers. He had Travis playing a different position, which he hated. There were other confrontations as well.

He called me one day, "Mom, I'm going to complete this semester, but I don't want to finish here."

"Son, you've never been away from home before, you have to give it a chance. You can't just leave the school whenever you want to. We have a lot of money invested in your education there."

"Can you talk to Dad, please?"

"No, T, you can talk to Dad. The rest will be Dad's decision. I understand what you're saying, but sometimes we have to do what we don't want to. That's just part of life, and we don't quit in the middle. You've never been a quitter, so don't start now."

He talked to Jeff. He wanted Travis to stay and finish out the year, but in the end, Travis was determined to finish the semester and come home.

I called Eckerd College. We had looked at a Eckerd, which was located in St. Petersburg, when Travis was still in high school. It had not been one of his choices, but they had a good basketball program. He applied and got a partial basketball scholarship. He liked the coach and settled well into his classes.

Jeff had not been happy about Travis leaving Florida Southern. Although he wasn't pleased that he had changed Travis to a different position, he liked the coach there. The coach was so upset that Travis was going over to Eckerd that he tried to ban Travis from playing basketball there because they were in the same NCAA Division. We felt the coach knew how much talent he had and didn't want him to be competition. In the end, the coach gave his release, but the season was over.

Jeff was continuing to have trouble going up and down the stairs at the house, so we decided to put it up for sale. We didn't really need a house that big anymore. I had kept my real estate license active and listed it myself.

The pain management clinic that Jeff's family doctor recommended seemed to be working out. He wasn't binging as much, and at his request, I was helping him regulate his meds. Because of that he would blame me for trying to control his life. I didn't like it because it always put me in the mother-caretaker role, instead of the wife-lover role.

But for now, we were getting along. We started looking around and went to a few open houses. It was nice to be doing something together and being a team.

Our house had only been on the market for a few months in February 2004, when a buyer knock on my front door.

"Hi, my name is Joan. I know your flyer said that you require a 24-hour notice, but I'm only in town for a few days visiting my daughter, son-in-law and grandson who live around the corner."

Even though I was home alone, there was something about her. "No problem, Joan, come on in. I'm Brandi Winans. Where are you visiting from?"

"Colorado. I used to live in Miami and I have five sisters and one brother who all live in Orlando. My daughter is expecting again, so I'm thinking about living here part of the year."

We hit it off immediately, so I invited her to see the movie, The Passion of the Christ, the following day, with another girlfriend, Annie.

After the movie, Annie had to leave, so Joan and I ate a late lunch. During that time, she told me she wanted to buy the house and we negotiated the deal at lunch. I just needed Jeff's approval. Jeff agreed to the terms although the offer was less than the asking price, but we wanted her to have the house.

We would close in sixty days, that would give us time to find a place to live. Travis helped me pack as Jeff was getting ready to have another knee surgery.

A week after we signed the contract, Joan called. "I found a great rate but to keep it I need to close by the end of the month."

We didn't want the deal to fall through so we bumped up the closing date. That put a lot of stress on me to get all the packing done. As soon as I hung up the phone, my emotions started to run wild. It was harder than I thought it was going to be to leave this house. We thought we were going to be here the rest of our lives. It was the house where we had our roots for sixteen years. This was where Travis grew up. A lot of good and bad memories were here, but it was home. I knew I had to get past this and start packing. It hit Jeff just as hard–especially right after the knee surgery. Wanting to back out of the deal, we realized we needed to move on.

Jeff found a house to rent, almost immediately, in a subdivision near the beaches where I had grown up. We signed a nine-month lease, so there was no going back. That would give us time to find something else.

The move just about killed me. Jeff was still on crutches. Jeff always said I didn't live in his body, but then he didn't live in mine.

Although the pain medication the doctors had him on seemed to be working, within a few months of the move Jeff lost close to thirty pounds and his memory loss was getting more and more noticeable. That would trigger confusion which would turn to anger and then an argument. I would accuse him of taking too much medication and passing out. It never occurred to me that he could be having black-outs.

The pain management clinic continued to do a number of expensive back and neck procedures. Our prescription drug bill was now almost $2,000 a month.

Even though Jeff was on anti-depressants, his depression and headaches were still there. He would say things like, "You know I don't have very long to live." He was either living for, "When this happens. I'll be happy when," or constantly talking about the past. It was never the now. It was never, "Let's make today happy. Let's be together and go do something."

He would have good intentions, but never seemed able to follow through, and as he became more distant I got more involved in my charity work and seminars.

I had been running errands all day and stopped at the grocery store on the way home. As I sat the groceries down on the kitchen counter, I could here Jeff snoring profusely. I walked down the hall and stood at the bedroom door. He was spread eagle on the bed–one shoe on one shoe off. The evidence of prescription bags was in the trash can beside the bed. He had picked up his prescriptions and had taken God-only-knows how many. The actual prescription bottles were nowhere in sight.

I felt my blood pressure shoot up as my heart started to pound. I was a volcano about to erupt. I went in to the kitchen, picked up the phone and called his doctor at the pain management clinic. I told the front office that Jeff had taken a lot of his medication and I demanded to speak to the doctor.

Dr. Hassan got on the phone and I gave him an earful. "Jeff is passed out on the bed and snoring! May I ask what prescriptions you prescribed for him today?" I was on a roll. "Are you also aware that Jeff is on anti-depressants and that he was diagnosed as bipolar, with manic depression and borderline personality disorder?"

He wasn't aware of anything. "Can you bring him to my office in the morning?"

"Yes, Dr. Hassan, just give me a time and I'll be there."

When Jeff woke up later that evening, I told him I had spoken to his doctor and he wanted to see him in the morning.

He said, angrily, "Why would you do that? You always have to ruin it for me!"

"I love you, but I can't take living like this anymore. As your wife, I have a right to know what he gave you. He said he wasn't going to give you Valium anymore and he gave it to you anyway."

I slept in the guest room and the next morning, I drove him to the doctor's office.

As we walked in, Dr. Hassan said, "Jeff, I hear you have been a very bad boy."

Jeff was silent, and looked over at me like he could kill me. He sat at one end of the room and I sat at the other. Dr. Hassan was in the middle at his desk with his back to us, reviewing Jeff's file. Jeff gave me that black-eye stare, then flipped me the finger.

Dr. Hassan turned around, "Your wife tells me that you're abusing your drugs. From looking at you today, I believe her. I'm going to have you give me a urine sample. Jeff, you only get one chance with us. These are very powerful drugs. My license is on the line. Do you understand?"

"Yes," he said, looking at the doctor like some scolded child.

Dr. Hassan looked at both of "Here's what we will do from now on. Your wife will be in charge of your medication. She will dispense it to you at the designated times. You'll take a random drug test when you come for your monthly visits. That's the only way we'll continue this relationship. If not, I will not be able to see you anymore. I want a written diagnosis from Dr. Mayo explaining what she is treating you for, before your next visit. You never told me you were on any other medication. Is that agreeable with you?"

"Yes," he replied.

"I'm going to change one of your medications because you should not be taking Valium with Lithium and Wellbutrin XL. I'm going to give you a non-narcotic muscle relaxer for your spasms. You can continue to take the Soma for now."

The doctor looked at me. "Mrs. Winans, are you willing to do this for your husband?"

Jeff was glaring at me. I wanted to say, "No. We've tried this before and all he does is bully and badger until he gets what he wants." Instead, I said, "Yes," Dr. Hassan. I'll give it a try and see how it works out." I wanted to say no, I've been doing this for years but the mood Jeff was in and the consequences were too much.

As Dr. Hasson turned around to write his report, those black ice cold stares were upon me and Jeff gave me the middle finger again. The ride home was not pleasant. Jeff felt betrayed.

He said, coldly, "How could you turn on me? How could you do this to me? Don't you understand the kind of pain that I'm in?"

I kept silent as I was driving us home and kept flashing back to different times in our marriage. I went back a few years back when I thought I was having a heart attack. I was helping Academy Prep put on their first golf tournament. Jeff and I had been fighting about all the drugs he was taking. I had been feeling a lot of pressure on my chest for a few days, and at times felt like I couldn't breathe.

The next morning, it was worse. I thought if I got dressed and out of the house, it may go away. I took a couple of Tums. It didn't. I called Susan, (the gal I was working on the tournament with) and told her I wasn't feeling well. I asked her to meet me at St. Anthony's Emergency Room. She was waiting for me when I pulled up.

I got out, opened my trunk, and gave her all of the golf stuff: signs, cash box, registration sheets, and the rest, and told her I would be there in a few hours. I reassured her that she could do this until I arrived. I left praising her with the confidence she needed.

I parked the car and went up to the fourth floor to see my family doctor. My heart was pounding; I was in a cold sweat. I found out after walking into his office that he was on vacation and his nurse quickly escorted me down the hall to another doctor who was on call for him that week. When we walked in, the nurse took one look at me, rushed me into the examining room, and had me lay down on a gurney. The young doctor came in and immediately gave me a vile of amyl nitrate.

After taking my vitals she said, "Mrs. Winans, you are not going anywhere. I think you are having a heart attack and I'm going to admit you."

"You can't!" I said frantically, "I'm putting on a golf tournament today and I promised them I'd be there in a few hours."

She shook her head, "We'll you're not. Where is your husband? We need to notify him."

They called Jeff, and by the time he got there, I was in my hospital room waiting to go for some more testing.

He was concerned and very upset, then as the day went on, and he found out that I might not have had a heart attack, his mood turned to anger. He started accusing me of making this all up for attention. I started crying. How could he think I would possibly make up something as serious as this? Heart attacks ran in my family.

One of the nurses overheard Jeff's loud voice and came into my room. She saw how upset I was and asked Jeff to leave. She stayed with me as I balled like a little baby. Why did he have to act like this when I was in need? The nurse gave me a sedative to calm me down and I fell asleep.

A few hours later, Jeff and Travis showed up. Jeff brought flowers and a card for me. His whole personality had changed. Travis was very concerned, too, because he had never seen me in a hospital before.

When they were leaving, Jeff walked over and whispered in my ear, "I'm sorry. I love you. I got scared that something bad was going to happen to you."

I was apprehensive about believing him. "It's all right. I'm going for a stress test in the morning and if everything is okay I can go home tomorrow. My other tests should be back by then. I don't want us to argue."

I came home the next afternoon. It turned out I had a panic attack. A panic attack? I had always been the strong one. My family doctor put me on some medication that I took only whenever I felt an attack coming on. Exercise helped a lot because it boosted my endorphins. But sometimes, nothing helped and I would revert to the medication for a few days.

Today, it was the drama with Dr. Hasson. A few days later, Jeff's anger toward me subsided. He could see my frustration and said he was going to try harder.

The next week together was great. It was my birthday and Jeff said he wanted to take me out to dinner to celebrate. We had an appointment to look at a house and scheduled it around five-thirty, just before dinner.

Jeff was in a great mood and after being seated at our table, ordered a double martini, up, and I ordered a glass of wine. The conversation started out great as he toasted my birthday. It went downhill from there.

"We're getting along pretty well today," he said, "wouldn't you agree?"

"Yes, honey, and this is a special treat for you to take me out to dinner today. Why?"

"Because we have a lot to talk about. I'm still waiting for you to tell me the truth."

"The truth about what?" I was confused.

"I just want you to start being honest with me."

I assumed he was talking about his meds and my tattling on him.

"You and Travis are always plotting against me. You're only here for my money." I realized then it wasn't about the meds.

"Jeff, we don't plot against you."

"No," he said, "you just hide things from me." Paranoia was setting in.

"What have we hidden from you now? And it's our money, Jeff. Every dime I ever made went into our joint accounts. I have never, in all the years I worked to support us, said that this was "my" money, or when I inherited what was left of my Mother's estate."

"We were married and I was entitled to her money. I helped her all the time."

"No," I said, "you weren't. Inheritance is not community property unless it's co-mingled. I could have taken all of that money and opened up a separate "selfish" account, but we used it to remodel the house. Why are you doing this on my birthday? Can we please just enjoy our meal?"

"Fine, Brandi. It always about you, isn't it?"

I kept silent. I could see where it was going and I didn't want to provoke it anymore. Our dinner came and he had two more double Martinis. No matter what I said, he had a nasty comeback.

We paid the check and left. Halfway home on the interstate, he started in on me again. I knew it was the combination of the booze and drugs, so I tried to stay calm. He had episodes before where he would get violent and get in my face. Then he would hit and break something. Several times he put holes in the walls. Sometimes it was with his fist.

He looked over at me in the car and started yelling. I didn't respond. I kept quiet. I could see the fire in his eyes and the expression on his face. We were in a very confined space in the car.

"Brandi, let me out of the f—ing car! Right now!!"

I knew I had to stay calm. "Honey, I'm going 70 miles an hour. I can't let you out. I'll let you out as soon as I get to the exit."

"I'm warning you, Brandi, if you don't pull this car over right now, I'm going to rip your f—ing head off!!"

He was serious. He was shaking and his face was purple with rage. All I could do was drive.

I said, calmly, "Honey, we're almost to a point where we can get off the freeway and if you still want me to let you out, I will."

"I don't care where we are, just pull over the f—ing car and let me out or I mean it, Brandi, I will rip you f—ing head off!!!"

The next thing I knew, he lunged toward me with his left hand and let out a loud groan. I put my right arm up by my face with my elbow towards his arm. Just as I braced myself, he pulled back his hand and grabbed the rear view mirror. With another loud groan, he ripped the mirror out of the windshield. The windshield cracked. There were wires hanging out of it. He looked at me, then the rearview mirror, and threw it in the backseat. He started pounding his fist on the dashboard.

"See what you made me do!" he shouted.

I was surprised that the air bag hadn't released. He started screaming at me again. His body was still shaking. I knew I had to remain calm. If I showed any emotion, I was afraid he would kill me and not realize what he had done. Under my breath, I was praying for God to help me.

We were almost home when we got off the exit, so I decided to keep driving. There was silence in the car as I pulled into the driveway and stopped. My hands were still shaking and my heart was pounding as he got out and slammed the car door.

I was afraid to go in the house because he might become violent again. So I called my girlfriend and drove over to her house on the beach. For the first time in our relationship, I was truly afraid of him. I didn't know where Travis was, but his bedroom was a separate suite off the back side of the house. I called him on his phone. He didn't answer, which usually meant he was out. I was afraid that Jeff would go in and pick a fight with him.

The car broke down the next day while I was running some errands. A lot of the computer stuff that ran the car was in the front windshield. I called and asked Jeff to come pick me up and waited for AAA to tow the car to the dealer.

As soon as Jeff arrived he said, "Brandi, I'm so sorry for the way I treated you yesterday. You didn't deserve that. No one deserved to be treated like that. Everything I have been holding in came out. I'll get the car fixed."

"What are you going to tell them?'

"The truth."

"You're going to tell them what you did?"

"Yes."

"We can't keep going on like this, Jeff."

"I know, Brandi. I'm going to quit cold turkey again."

"You've tried that before. It's never worked. Why don't you talk to your doctors and let them recommend a facility where you can get the proper treatment. They have so many great medications to help wean you off so you don't have to go through the withdrawals."

"I have to do this by myself."

Mother's Day was in a few days and we celebrated each year with family and friends. This year, the dinner was to be at our house and I had about twenty-five people coming over.

Jeff had started withdrawals the day before and it was his worst day. We closed the blinds and bedroom door in the master bedroom, and he got under the covers to sweat it out. I put a garbage can by his bed for him to throw up in, if necessary.

Jeff rarely came to family/friend functions, he was uncomfortable. If he did come, he would stay for an hour and leave–so we would usually drive in separate vehicles. Everyone wanted to know where Jeff was when they came in. I told them he had a bout of the flu and was lying down, so he wouldn't be joining us. They accepted my answer and Mother's Day went off without a hitch.

I would check on him every half hour. Travis didn't have a clue. It was just routine, and he loved his Dad so much and accepted him the way he was because of everything he had been through.

We got through the next week. Two days after Jeff went through all of the withdrawals, he was back on the Duragesic patches. His irrational behavior was becoming more and more noticeable.

I felt so helpless in all of this trying to do the right thing. I wondered how long I could continue to cover up for him. But the enabler, the caretaker and the love I had for him couldn't let go.

Chapter 27

My Turn

Travis decided to get an apartment with two of his best friends from high school and moved out.

A few weeks after Mother's Day, I was at an Athletes and Executives luncheon in Tampa. I was late, so I slipped in the side door and literally bumped into an old friend, Hal Jeffrey. Hal was the Chaplain for the Bucs when Jeff played there. We exchanged cards and a few days later he called. He said was going to do a radio show in Texas on the Family Radio Channel.

Hal worked with professional athletes who were making the transition back to society after their careers in sports were over. He asked me if I would be interested in doing a ten minute segment on his show about what it's like being the spouse of a pro athlete. He wanted to meet for breakfast and discuss another alternative, about something that would be coming to Tampa. We met for breakfast the next day.

"Brandi, I know you have a passion for the teens and young adults and parents. Would you be interested in doing a weekly radio show? I would produce it and bring in sponsors and book your guest speakers. I put some numbers together, and we could make a decent income off the advertising spots and sponsors we get to pay for the show and our salaries. I have an in with WTBN Christian Talk Radio Station in Tampa and I have worked with them before."

"Let me take a look at this Hal and I'll get back with you. It sounds great. I have to figure out what kind of show I would want to do and talk it over with Jeff. Give me a few days."

"No problem. Just don't wait too long. There are only a few slots available where I think we could draw a good audience."

I talked to Jeff and told him about the opportunity. He was not fond of Hal. There had been a problem between them when Jeff was president of the NFL Alumni.

I met with the station manager and operation manager of WTBN to make sure everything was on the up and up. After that, Jeff approved and the show was a go. We would start in August and I would call it, "Parents Talk Teens Rap." That would give us a few months to get some sponsors and advertisers.

After Travis moved out, Jeff and I decided to really work on our marriage and look for another house to buy.

Off and on for the last eight years, after I stopped boxing, I would get these strange rushes of numbness that would start at the top of my head and run down to my torso. Within a few seconds, I would be totally numb. I had tried to ignore them, but now they were getting more and more frequent, so I finally went to see a neurologist.

I was scared, especially with everything we had been through with Jeff. He was always having a surgery, or something, so I felt my needs weren't that important. After three MRIs, my neurologist, Dr. Kramer, called and asked both of us to come in. I prayed for two days for healing and the strength to get through whatever the end result would be. His nurse seemed very upbeat as we walked down the hall to an examining room. Dr. Kramer came in and sat down.

"Hello, Jeff it's nice to finally meet you. Brandi, I have some good news and some bad news. I took Jeff's hand. The good news is that you don't have a brain tumor or multiple sclerosis. You do, however, have something we call a syrinx, which is a hole in your spinal cord. There are two ways that this usually happens: one, you are born with it or two, it is created from trauma to the brain and spinal cord."

"What does this mean, doc? Do I have to have surgery?" I asked with apprehension.

"Well, that's the bad news, Brandi. There is nothing that we can do. You can live a very normal life as long as you don't experience any further trauma to the head or neck–at which point you could become paralyzed. Obviously, you don't box anymore. I'll want to monitor your syrinx by having an MRI every few years, or if you start experiencing dizziness, get nauseous or anything out of the ordinary. Do you have any further questions?"

"No, Dr. Kramer, thank you for being so honest. Now that I know what it is and, as you said, it's not a brain tumor or multiple sclerosis, I can deal with it."

"The other thing I have to tell you is that I am leaving the practice here and moving to the other coast. I love it here, but it's personal. We'll be renting our house out. We just bought it, so if you know of anyone who may be interested, let me know."

Jeff and I looked at each other and decided to drive by and take a look. Maybe we could rent his home and wait to buy something later. After driving by and seeing that Dr. Kramer's house was a two-story, and not what we were looking for, we drove around the corner and saw another house for sale by owner. We decided to call and make an appointment. It was a Frank Lloyd Wright looking house with two apartments in the back, over four garages. It was very unique.

We both loved the house, but it was way above our budget. I didn't want us to get in the same situation we had gotten into before, and then live above our means.

Jeff had other ideas. "I want this house, Brandi, and I'm gonna buy it. We can afford the monthly payments!"

There was no arguing with him. This is how we had bought the other two houses. In other words, he didn't care what I thought. I just had to figure out how to make it work. He knew somehow that I always did, and I was still afraid of him, so I allowed it to happen.

We set the closing for August 16, 2004. I had a lot to do over the next few months and a lot of packing, again. About a month after we got the house under contract, Jeff called me into our bedroom. He was lying on the bed with his prosthetic off. I could see from the look on his face something was wrong.

"Can you take a look at this?"

I looked down at his right leg and saw that he had another infection. His stump was swollen just below the knee and it was purple red. There was puss draining out of the infamous old black hole where the bullet had originally entered from the gunshot accident.

"It looks like you have a major infection. I'll call Dr. Williams (our infectious specialist) and tell him you have to see him today".

As much as we argued, whenever there was a crisis, it seemed to bring us back together. People tend to forget what the spouse of someone with physical or emotional problems goes through. They only see what the person going through the situation is facing.

Dr. William's office was able to get us in right away. I put some Neosporin on his wound, then wrapped and taped his leg, grabbed his crutches from the closet, and we were on our way.

Upon our arrival, Dr. William's nurse took us directly to an examining room. We told her Jeff's leg was infected again and very swollen. She carefully cut the bandages off to exam the stump. She barely touched the surrounding area of the leg to exam it when his leg literally exploded. Blood was spurting out everywhere like a garden hose, spattering all over the front of her uniform.

She ran out of the examining room door and called for help. Dr. Williams ran in. Jeff's blood was still spurting out everywhere; on the walls, on the floor. No one had ever seen this happen before. It was total chaos. Dr. Williams grabbed a white towel and quickly wrapped Jeff's leg, and started applying direct pressure. Jeff was in excruciating pain.

Dr. Williams looked at his nurse "Call St. Anthony's emergency room now and notify them that he's coming!"

"Mrs. Winans, we need to get him over there now. It will be quicker if you drive him."

"No problem, doc."

We got Jeff into the car and I drove him cross the street to the ER. They were waiting for us. They got him out of the car and onto a gurney and wheeled him inside. Dr. Williams was there in a matter of minutes and Jeff was taken into emergency surgery.

Apparently, over the years, when he would have an infection, there was some that never got completely out of his system. It finally had become septic and the black hole that I used to have to pack with gauze finally erupted.

After the surgery, Dr. Williams said, "I have never seen so much stuff in one condensed area. We cleaned it out. He should never get that kind of infection again. He's going to be on crutches for about six weeks and should have a full recovery."

It seemed like every time he was surgery free, something would come back and haunt us, but somehow like today, God always came through.

Chapter 28

Lady Luck Shows Up

Jeff was recovering well from his infectious surgery and August 2004 was here before we knew it. We closed on the new house (which we were going to remodel and not move into until October) and I launched my radio show on WTBN Christian Talk 570 & 910am Radio in Tampa.

There was a hurricane brewing out in the Gulf of Mexico. We were still at the house near the beach and surrounded by water. Four days later, the hurricane in the gulf was headed right for the Tampa Bay area. We evacuated the rental house and stayed with Cookie and Linda, old friends who lived in Bellaire, Florida.

Then Lady Luck showed up. Just before the hurricane was scheduled to hit Tampa Bay, it turned. Still, the storm brought sustained winds of up to 100 miles per hour, and a lot of wind damage. We were very blessed it had not been a direct hit. There was little damage to either house. Within the next two-week period, three more hurricanes, including Hurricane Katrina, were upon us. Never, in all my years of growing up here had there been such catastrophic damage in the south.

As much as we were trying to make things work, it wasn't long before the radio show started to put a strain on Jeff and me. Several times I invited Jeff to come on the show with me so he could see what we were doing and he declined. Instead of being happy for me that we were trying to reach out and help people, he got more and more lost inside his medication.

I couldn't get him to understand that we had sponsors who were paying for everything, and we would argue over money. He wasn't in control of the show or me when I was away from the house doing my Wannabe Seminars or youth ministry at the church, and that brought on his insecurities. In his mind, I always had some ulterior motive. Rather than argue with him anymore, I would say, "I'm sorry that you feel that way." I decided that I wasn't going to allow him to steal my joy. I couldn't make him happy. Happiness is a choice. That had to come from within.

Travis decided to take a year off from college and become a personal trainer. He worked hard over the next six months and earned two personal training certifications. He decided to work at the local Gold's Gym where he had been working out. Jeff wanted him to stay in school at that point. I supported his need to leave school and that created more conflict between us.

After the remodel was completed, we moved into the new house the end of October 2004. We loved the Frank Lloyd Wright Style '50s contemporary style home. The back yard looked like something out of the garden of paradise with a waterfall pond, swimming pool, several fountains and so much flora and fauna, on a third of an acre corner lot. The inside part of the house was full of character–with tons of wood and glass block, high ceilings, a glass wall that overlooked the pond and a gourmet kitchen.

We were one block from Lassing Park, which was a twelve and a half acre park on the water. Jeff was upbeat and happy, with a workshop in one of the four garages.

A few months after we moved in, I stopped in to see an old friend of mine, TW, who had recently opened an art gallery in downtown St. Petersburg. While I was there, a gentleman walked past me, carrying a painting. He was putting up a display in one of the corners of the gallery.

"Brandi," TW said, "I want to introduce you to my friend, Jeff Belyea. Jeff is a new artist and writer in the area and I've just added him to our gallery roster of artists.

"It's so nice to meet you."

I noticed a stack of books that seemed to be part of the display that he was putting together. One of his paintings was used on the book's cover design. I picked up one of the books and quickly recognized that it was a "spiritual" book and asked if I could purchase one. He was delighted to have a book sale before he had even put his display up in his new gallery.

'Where are you from,' I asked as I paid for the book.

"Maine. My wife is still up there and will be joining me in a few months. In the meanwhile, I need to find an apartment for a while. I just came into St. Petersburg today."

"How long do you need a place for?"

"Until May, about four months."

"How long have you been an artist and writer?"

"Most of my life–since I was very young."

He went on to tell me that he had a PHD in communications, was certified in hypnotherapy, and had been a pastor at a church in Maine for seven years. He also mentioned that his wife was a yoga teacher and licensed massage therapist.

I had a good feeling about him right away. When I heard that he was a former pastor, I invited him to be a guest on my radio show. And I had another surprise in store for him.

"Jeff, we have a house and two apartments over four garages. My husband and I have thought about renting them out for the season. I need to talk to him and if agrees, I'll see if we can let you use one of garages so your car won't be on the street."

All I had to do was convince my Jeff. After explaining to him how I met Dr. Belyea, and that his wife would be joining him in a few months, Jeff agreed to let him move in. Susan Belyea's parents rented a condo on Madeira Beach until May, and then the Belyea's were going to move there.

Jeff moved in the following week. It was nice to have company. He and my Jeff hit it off. Shortly thereafter, Jeff decided to go off his anti-depressants. Even his psychiatrist was reluctant and wanted him to at least stay on the Lithium. Jeff didn't see it that way. He felt he was well enough to handle it.

Within a few weeks, his mood swings were back worse than before, and he turned to taking even more of his medications. I became embarrassed and it was hard to cover up and protect him. In April 2005, a month after Jeff Belyea moved in, I came home from the radio station around nine-thirty. It had been a long day. I walked in the back door through the kitchen and found Jeff was snoring in front of the TV. I went over to my chair, sat down and said hi to the dogs.

Jeff heard my voice and woke up. I said hello, then proceeded to go in the bedroom to change clothes. When I came out, Jeff was gone. I assumed he had gone outside to have a cigarette.

About ten-fifteen, I went out to check on him. He had put a TV in the workshop in the garage. Sometimes if he was smoking, he would sit out there. I went outside and peeked in the garage. The TV was on but there was no Jeff. I came back in the house. Then it hit me, something wasn't right. I checked the front patio by the front door. He wasn't there either. I called his name several times. I went to the back yard again. Then I heard a moan.

Frantically I said, "Jeff, Jeff, where are you?"

I followed his moans. He was too high on medication to speak. I found him in the bushes in the backyard near the back bedroom. He had lost his balance and fallen. When he fell, he fell on a brick that was turned sideways. We had taken some extra bricks and made brick planters to match the brick walkways. It was dark and I couldn't see very well. I ran over and turned on the back patio lights. He was bleeding and in a lot of pain. There still wasn't enough light to see all of his leg and I couldn't get him up without some help.

"Jeff you're going to have to help me get you up. You are too heavy and I can't do this by myself."

We both struggled and somehow I got him up. He couldn't put any weight on the left leg.

"Sit back down, I'm going to call an ambulance."

"No!" he said, shaking his head.

"Then let me see if Jeff Belyea is home."

"No!

"All right, let's get you to the steps so I can see in the light what kind of damage you've done."

I put my arm around him and he put his weight on me. I guess

I had more adrenalin than I thought. Somehow, we made it to the steps. It was his left knee. It was cut wide open.

"Oh God, Jeff. You need stitches. We need to get you to the hospital now!"

I thought I heard, "Okay." It was hard to understand him. I ran in the house and grabbed my purse and a towel for his leg. My adrenaline was still flowing. I was angry at him, because this type of accident could have been avoided.

We got to the closest hospital, in a matter of minutes and I pulled up to the Emergency doors. Jeff was coming in and out of consciousness from all the medication he had taken earlier. They helped him out of my car, put him on a gurney, and took him to an examining room. I filled out the paperwork. By now, I think our insurance was on file at every hospital in Pinellas County. I told the nurse that he had gotten a bottle of thirty 10mg Valiums that day, but I didn't know how many he had taken because I just got home from work.

It seemed to take forever before they let me back to see him when I realized why it was taking so long. I could hear him snoring all the way down the hall. Great, the infamous Winans snore. As I walked into his room, one of the nurses was taking his vitals. She looked up at me. I smiled. She smiled back.

Embarrassed, I jokingly said, "Well, I guess he hasn't overdosed yet."

She smiled again. "His heart rate is up, but his breathing is fine. The doctor will be in shortly."

A few minutes later, the doctor on duty came in.

"Mrs. Winans?" (I was beginning to think that every doctor in St. Pete knew my name).

"Yes."

"What has your husband taken?"

"As far as I know, he got a new script for thirty 10mg Valium about three this afternoon from his psychiatrist. I do a radio show from eight to nine. He wasn't feeling any pain when I left the house about half past six. I found the empty bottle in the garbage can before I left to do the show. He always takes them and hides them so I won't know how many he's taken."

The doctor looked at Jeff's knee. "Mr. Winans, wake up. You're in the hospital. Mr. Winans can you hear me?"

Jeff slowly opened one eye, then the other.

"Mr. Winans, can you tell me what happened?"

Jeff tried to talk, but it was all gibberish. I told the doctor what had happened and how distraught I was over his behavior–how helpless I felt watching someone constantly self-destruct.

He examined his knee, and cleaned it out. "Do you have an orthopedic doctor that you'd like me to call?"

"Why?"

"Because it looks like Jeff has torn the patella tendon in his knee and he'll need surgery, so I can't sew him up."

He could see that I was still very distraught.

"We have a psychologist on hospital staff. Would you like me to call him?"

My mouth started to tremble. I really did need to talk to someone.

"Yes, doc, I don't know what to do and I can't keep living like this anymore. He's like a little four year old that you can't leave alone."

"I'll call our psychologist, Dr. Law, and I'll call Dr. Smith and give him a heads up."

He looked at Jeff. "Jeff, Jeff, can you hear me?"

Jeff was snoring again. I tried to smile but my bottom lip started to tremble again.

"For now we're going to let him sleep it off here. When he's more coherent, we'll move him into the orthopedic ward on the fourth floor. I'll have Dr. Smith's office give you a call regarding surgery."

The nurse came in a few minutes later and said the shrink was ready to see me. At that point, I was ready to go home and not say anything, but when I found out that he driven over to see me, I felt obligated.

I spoke with the hospital psychologist for about an hour. They always want to know your life story. It was basically the same answer all the other shrinks had given me. I have a choice. I can stay or I can move out and move forward in my life. It's not that easy when you love someone. He gave me his card and said if Jeff would like to get some help, to call him.

It was now about one in the morning. I decided not to go back to see Jeff, and headed home. Once home, I became obsessed with finding the rest of his pills. In my haste, I accidentally locked the door to the workshop garage and had to open it with a screwdriver and a credit card. I spent another hour going through the house and garages, only to find nothing. Frustrated, I sat down in the workshop and cried.

I called Dr. Smith's office the next morning and found out that Jeff was scheduled for surgery that afternoon. Then I called Travis to let him know what had happened in case he wanted to see his father.

The surgery was a success and Jeff had to wear a special brace on his leg for the next six to eight weeks. He was very lucky. He wasn't able to bend his leg for that length of time, so the tendon could heal. When I went to bring him home from the hospital, he asked me where the rest of his valium was and we got into a big argument. He said he lost his balance and fell and it had nothing to do with the number of Valium he had taken.

A few weeks after Jeff got out of the hospital, I was cleaning my car and found a chrome pill case under the carpet in the passenger's side. Inside the pill case was fifteen of the thirty 10 mg. valium he had picked up at the pharmacy the day he fell. I dumped them down the toilet and told Jeff what I had done. He was not happy about it and accused me having had them all along.

There were humorous events that happened along the way. Jeff couldn't drive a car for eight weeks. He had to rely on me for every-thing–showers, food, buying his diet coke and cigarettes (which at times I wanted to hold for ransom because I wanted him to quit). We also had to remove the cabinet in the master bathroom so he could sit down on the toilet.

After his leg started to heal and the brace was off, I started to spend more and more time upstairs in the other apartment. When we moved into the new house, I needed an office. . Jeff didn't like people in the house that he didn't know. One of the apartments over the garage was perfect. It had a den that I used as my office. If I had to conduct any business with clients, we could just go up to the apartment and not bother Jeff.

We seemed to be living two different lives. But after being together so many years, there was a comfort zone there, too. We never had a normal marriage. Most people and families didn't have to deal with the intense physical and emotional problems, the NFL, lawsuits, bankruptcy, multiple operations, and hospital stays. At times I felt like a failure because I couldn't keep it all together. Then one day shortly after leaving the house the Holy Spirit came all over me in the car.

God said to me, "Daughter, you are not in control. I am. I don't need your help. Let me release you from this burden you have been trying to carry all by yourself."

Over the last few years of finding God again, I had started to give over control, but had never let it go completely. I can't explain it, other than at that moment I let go, let God, and made the effort to give this burden back to Him.

I realized that I wasn't in control of Jeff or Travis's destiny. This was the day it finally sunk in. I could be the best that I could be, continue my work, reach out and start enjoying my life. Although I wanted Jeff to be a part of it, I couldn't make him. That's why we are given free will. The only person I could change was me.

A few days later, I got a call from Hazel Hudson. She was with the Charles Britt Halfway House in St. Petersburg. Charles Britt Halfway House is a six to eighteen month moderate risk residential prison for young men. Hazel headed up the faith-based Community Initiative. She said that Jim Needs, the former assistant superintendent at the Pinellas Juvenile Detention Center (JDC), had referred her to me. She asked if I would be interested in doing my Wannabe Seminars at the Britt House. I met with her the following week and started working with the teens a few weeks later. It was what I needed to keep my mind off my own troubles. God works in mysterious ways. The seminars and the radio show kept me very busy.

Jeff was his skeptical self. "How much are we getting paid for this one?"

"Jeff, I know you don't understand but I am sowing seeds. These kids need help. They are the future of this country."

"And you're here to save the world."

"I can't explain it to you. You have done so much through our foundation to help and give to kids in need, why can't you understand this?" I had to let it go.

Travis was doing well and would come over for Sunday dinners. The tension between Jeff and me was nothing new for him. He decided he wanted to go back to school in the fall. I was proud that it was his decision. Maybe now he would actually study. I knew, like all of us, he must grow in his own time and in his own way. I think as a parent, that's the hardest thing to learn. They have to go through their own growth spurts of life by themselves and experience the good, the bad and the ugly.

As a mother and protector, it's hard to let go, but knowing that God is in control of my son's destiny, and that he had been brought up a Christian, made it a little easier.

Chapter 29

Moving out

The new patio on our back yard was finally done. My girlfriend's husband gave us a really good deal on all of his labor, because we bought all the materials. I found a nature paver pattern that we liked at Home Depot and they custom ordered it for us. We had tried planting grass, but it was very shaded in that spot, so we decided to put the patio there. This gave us a place to put all of the patio furniture we had before.

Things were moving along. The Belyea's asked to come back for a second winter season, and were getting ready to move back in for a few months. Travis got his Apex Personal Training Certification (his second certification) and was studying for his NASM. Jeff had recovered from his knee surgery, still in rehab, but was able to wear his prosthetic again. I was glad because we had made plane reservations a few months back for all of us to go to California for Christmas to visit his parents and Bill and Polly. It was already the end of October and Christmas would be here before we knew it.

Things seemed to be going well and I walked out of the house to take the dogs for their routine walk when I heard Jeff come out of the workshop. His mood swings continued to be more erratic. I thought he was coming over to go for a walk with us. Out of the blue, he started in on me in a bullying, intimidating tone of voice. I never knew what I was waking up to anymore. One day he was Dr. Jekyll and another day he was Mr. Hyde. This morning he made some critical remarks that were very demeaning and ugly. He knew how to hurt me; my heart started to pound and I could feel my blood pressure rise. It brought back the memories of my birthday the year before. This time I had enough and with the distance between us, I snapped back.

"Well, honey, this is the last time you'll have to worry about it, because when I come back from walking the dogs, I'll be moving out of the main house and into the upstairs apartment."

"Good!" Then he said more very demeaning things that I won't repeat.

I was shaking as I turned around, opened the side gate and walked down the sidewalk with the dogs. After I got down the street, I started to cool off. I was already starting to feel like I should apologize to keep the peace, but there was no excuse for the way he treated me. As soon we arrived home and opened the gate to the backyard to let the dogs in, he came out of his workshop and started in on me again.

"Just get your f—ing stuff out of my house!"

Where was all of this coming from? I wanted to start defending myself again, and then I stopped. I bit my lip and went into the house. It wasn't worth the argument.

He followed me. "Didn't you hear me? I said pack your shit and leave!!"

He was starting to get into a rage. A rage I had seen too many times. After the car incident, I didn't like to argue back. I humbled myself.

"I don't have enough space upstairs for all my things, so for now I'll pack my immediate things and leave the rest here."

"Where's my f—ing plane ticket to California? I'm going to go ahead and leave now!"

He was breathing heavily and sweat was pouring down his face. He walked over to our dresser, opened it up and started to pull things out of his drawers, throwing them on the bed.

"If you're leaving, I'll just wait until after you get back from California to move upstairs."

He looked at me with those black eyes. "No, just pack your shit and get the f—k out of my house now. I don't want you in here going through my things while I'm gone!"

He was starting to scare me again. Every time I tried to open a drawer to pack, he would get in my way. I walked over to the night stand on my side of the bed, opened up the drawer, and handed him his plane ticket. He jerked it out of my hand. Silence came over the room. I decided to get my things out of the bathroom until he was out of the bedroom. Within an hour, I was upstairs. I took Taz and Sasha, my dog and cat. He kept Butkis, his dog.

I was a nervous wreck, but I wouldn't give him the pleasure of knowing that. I sat down at the dining room table in the upstairs apartment and just fell apart. I didn't think it would have gone this far, but it did. I was officially out of the house. As an enabler, I felt remorse because I knew he was sick. As a woman who had been emotionally and verbally abused for twenty-six years, I felt relieved.

A few hours later, I went back to get a few things out of the refrigerator. I knocked on the back door. He didn't answer, so I walked in. It was very quiet. As I walked down the hall, I saw that the TV was on but no Jeff. I called out his name, but there was no response. I walked over and peeked into the master bedroom. He was sprawled out on the bed. At first, it didn't look like he was breathing. As I got closer, that infamous snore came out. I got my stuff out of the refrigerator. As I went out the back door and up the stairs, the enabler/protector in me wanted to go back, but for now I was doing the right thing for me.

The Belyea's were saddened to hear that we had separated, but like me, felt that I had done the right thing.

We decided not to say anything to Travis about the separation. We didn't want to spoil his trip to California for Christmas. Travis came over for Sunday dinners and I cooked or grilled out at the main house. I thought Jeff would realize what he was losing, but he only went deeper within himself. It went downhill from there and we decided to tell Travis that I had moved upstairs.

He didn't say a word, but his face said everything. He was torn. He loved his Dad. He loved me. He knew what we had been through. He was part of it. He wanted me to be happy. But he also knew someone had to look out for his Dad. I told him that as long as I was here, I would look in on his Dad. He looked down at me, gave me that big smile, a very tight bear hug, and left. I sat on the couch and prayed. God, was I doing the right thing?

Chapter 30

Back to Where He Once Belonged

Jeff and I got settled into a routine over the next few months. Every morning, I got up, took Taz downstairs, fed Butkis and Sasha, then the fish in the pond. Jeff would get up a little later, pour a diet coke and read the paper from start to finish. We would have some small talk, maybe events of the day and then one of us would walk the dogs.

Sometimes we would have lunch together and go to a movie or watch television at night if one of our favorite shows was on.

I became involved with the Youth Ministry at Pasadena Community Church where I grew up and where my Dad had taught Sunday school. The kids were great and I actually got Jeff to go to church with me a couple of times. During that time, I wrote and recorded an audio CD called, "The Stepping Stones of Life," geared toward teens, and young adults, as God directed my path.

Jeff and I talked several times about getting back together, but we could never come to terms. The only way I would even think about it would be if we had marriage counseling, and he agreed to drug rehab and get back on his bi-polar medicine. He didn't think he needed any of that. In his mind, I was still trying to control him. A couple of times he would ask me if I was dating anyone?

"Dating a man right now is not in my future. I'm still in love with you."

One night while I was over and we were watching TV together, he said, "I've decided after the house is sold, I'm going to move back to Turlock. I've lost all of my friends here since we stopped doing the golf tournaments."

He took me by surprise, but one thing was for sure, I couldn't fight for him anymore. I couldn't watch him die, and I felt that if I kept enabling him, it would just be a matter of time before he'd kill himself.

We put the house on the market the first week of March 2006. Three weeks later, it was under contract. It was starting to set in that this move was for real. Every time I thought about it, my heart sank. I had no idea where I was going to go, but I was already worried about his well-being.

A few weeks later, Joan, the gal we sold our old house to, called and asked me to lunch. We usually got together when she was in town. She was sorry to hear about Jeff and me. "Where are you going to go?"

"I honestly don't know, Joan. As we get closer to the closing, I'll look for something, why?"

"I have the house up for sale, mainly because it's empty so much when I'm gone and I hate the flat land here in Florida. Maybe we could work something out on a month to month".

"If I need to show the house," I said, "who knows it better than me? If something happens or if we have a storm, hurricane, I can secure everything. I couldn't afford to split the mortgage payment, but I could pay at least a third."

"Are you sure, Brandi? It would be a month to month and we'd draw up a contract."

"I'm sure and thank you, Joan. Thank you."

Now I knew where I was going. A few weeks later, I got a call from an old friend called and said they needed a real estate trainer for their Camp 443. God does work in mysterious ways. It was only six hours a week, but it would help take my mind off everything.

By May 2006, Jeff had lost about fifty pounds. He was emaciated– nothing more than skin and bones. The buyers ordered the home inspection and my brother, George, and his wife Pearl, had been over helping me get the house ready. There were leaks in both of the shower/tubs in the apartments. We had been at Home Depot all morning getting everything we needed for the repairs, before coming back to the apartments.

As I walked out of the front door of my upstairs apartment, I glanced down to my right to the pool area of the main house. I saw Jeff lying flat on his back with his head a few inches from the pool. He wasn't moving. We had seen him about forty-five minutes before. At that time, it appeared that he took some muscle relaxants but he was still coherent.

My heart sank. "Jeff!" I screamed. There was no response. "Oh my God!"

My brother and I rushed down the stairs to the screened door to the pool. It was locked. I called Jeff's name out again but there was no response. We ran up the stairs into the main house, through the family room, kitchen and dining room and out the sliding glass doors in the dining room, down another set of stairs to the pool area.

Jeff was alive but barely breathing. His cane was lying on the ground by the stairs. I didn't know if he had fallen or had a heart attack. Sue, Jeff Belyea's wife, heard the commotion and came down from her apartment to see if she could help. Pearl, my sister-in law, called 911.

The paramedics came within a few minutes. Jeff was still totally unresponsive. They asked if I knew what he had taken. I told them what I thought he had in the house, but I didn't know what or how many.

I searched the house, but as I said before, he was always very good at hiding his drugs. After taking his vitals and deciding which hospital they were going to take him to, they loaded him in the ambulance and sped away. I told George and Pearl to finish up, lock the doors and I would call them later.

Sue and I headed to the hospital in my car. When we got there, they said they would let me know when I could see him. Thirty minutes went by and I finally approached a nurse.

"What is the problem? I am his wife".

A charge nurse came out and took me into her office.

"Your husband became violent after he arrived and they had to put him in restraints. When they get him calmed down and get him stable, we'll let you go back".

She asked me about my situation, and knowing that his life was at stake, I told her everything. She was very sympathetic and told me about her husband who had been an alcoholic and that she had finally divorced him.

"I'll call you as soon as you can go back, okay?"

I went back to the waiting room where Sue was sitting and told her what happened.

"Brandi, you have to be strong and not give in to this. He made his choice."

"I know, and his choice has been so self-destructive. He needs help. I've never been able to compete with the drugs. He's always chosen them over me."

She took my hand, and squeezed it and gave me a reassuring smile.

A few minutes later, I was able to see Jeff. The nurse opened up the curtain. I gasped. It was heartbreaking to see him this way. His hands and feet were in restraints. His arms were above his head cuffed to the gurney. His legs were spread eagle and in restraints, too. There was blood on his forearms and blood on the gurney. I thought about our son and what it would do to him if he saw his father like this. His eyes were closed and he looked at peace. His ER Doctor walked up.

"Mrs. Winans?"

I turned around. "Yes."

As her eyes met mine, my bottom lip trembled and uncontrollable tears ran down my face.

"How is he?"

"Well, we almost lost him. His breathing was very shallow when he arrived, and we gave him a drug to help him come down. Upon giving him the injection, he woke up and became very violent. We had to restrain him and I gave him a shot of morphine to counteract the other drug. He's stable now. Tell me about your situation, Mrs. Winans. I understand this is a regular occurrence with him abusing his prescription drugs. He didn't try to kill himself, correct?"

"I don't think so, no."

I told her what the pain management doctors prescribed on a monthly basis: 100mg. Duragesic patches taken every two days, one-hundred 350mg. Soma, sixty 10mg. Valium, sixty Percaden and Oxycodone for breakthrough.

She just shook her head, didn't understand why they would prescribe such strong medications.

"He used to take Lithium and Wellbutrin XL with all this for his bi-polar and manic depression. He also smokes pot."

"You know, Mrs. Winans, it's just a matter of time before he kills himself."

The tears continued down my face. "I know. That's why we're separated. We've decided to file for divorce after our house sells and he's moving back to California."

"I'm going to take him for a CT scan to make sure he doesn't have any head trauma. If everything checks out you can come and pick him up in about five to six hours, or you can stay."

"No, I'm not going to stay. I'm going to go over to my brother's house."

I handed her my business card. "Call me at this number and let me know when he's ready to go home."

She looked at my card and then at me. "What do you do, Mrs. Winans?"

"I'm a motivational and inspirational speaker."

We just looked at each other and started laughing.

"You can see I've done wonders for him."

She smiled. "Yea, I can see that. It's always the ones who are closest to you that you have the hardest time reaching."

We looked at Jeff. His eyes were opening and he gave me one of those shit-eating grins and said "Hi." Then he closed his eyes and started the infamous snore.

I went to my brother's house to calm down. I thanked him and Pearl for all their help. They loved Jeff but knew what I had been going through for years. Five hours later, while I was still there, Jeff called.

"Where have you been?"

"I'm here at my brother's house."

"They've been trying to reach you."

"My cell phone hasn't rung."

"They released me to go home. Can you come pick me up?"

"I'm on my way."

When I pulled into the hospital parking lot, Jeff was sitting on the side of the curb. I couldn't believe they had released him before I got there. It was then that I realized he only had on his black Hanes underwear, his New Balance tennis shoes and white crew neck socks. He was so thin he could have been mistaken for a homeless person.

When he got into the car, I asked him if he had his release papers. He pulled them out of his sock and just stared out the window. No other words were spoken. He was not happy that I had left him there. After I pulled into the garage, he got out of the car and went inside the house. I went upstairs. I was so thankful that he was all right. It would have been a tough call to make to Travis.

Chapter 31

Good Memories

I started to look at the blessings in my life. I was so glad to have the training opportunity at the real estate office, and blessed to be moving back into our old house. With the separation now a reality, I would need some additional income.

At first, Jeff seemed scared by the overdose, but by the end of May, he was back into his old routine. He was also angry at me because my sister-in-law had called 911. He thought I had done it to be mean. He didn't want to hear that we called to save his life. He was still in so much denial.

I decided not to tell Travis about the latest episode. Travis and I always worried about Jeff. We constantly checked up on him, making sure he hadn't fallen or passed out somewhere. I was thankful that Travis didn't smoke or do drugs and was into taking care of his body. As a personal trainer, he worked out at the gym six days a week. I also knew how much he loved his father.

I took a hiatus from the radio show and started to work at the real estate office as their trainer at the end of May 2006. I was going down to the main house less and less. It didn't make sense to do everything for Jeff, especially the entire housekeeping, toilets, vacuuming, etc.

Jeff would nit-pick at me so much about how after all those years of marriage, this was all we had left. He seemed to forget about all the surgeries, the bankruptcy, the extensive medical bills, prescription drug bills, doctor, and hospital bills. Somehow, in his mind, I had now stolen all of his money.

I got so tired of listening to him that one day I just looked at him and said, "Why don't you and Travis just take everything. I'll keep my exercise equipment, the étagère, the oak wine rack, my small Native American collection and the gold flatware. You and Travis take the rest.

God showed me in the end, it was just stuff. I still had a lot of family photos and fond memories, and I told Jeff to go through and take whatever photos he wanted. I rented a storage unit for what little I had left from twenty-six years of being together.

Throughout our entire marriage, his trust issue became very erratic. After we got the house under contract, he packed his moving boxes and wrapped so much tape around them that Fort Knox couldn't have been more secure. He feared I would try and open them up. One morning, I came down to make breakfast for him and couldn't find any measuring cups.

When I was gone during the day or if I went out with my girlfriends, Jeff would come into my apartment, go through my drawers and take things he felt belonged to him. As I look back now, I don't think he remembered he took them. I continued to be more afraid of him, especially when he was high, so I started putting a dining room chair up against my doorknob every night to make sure he wouldn't come in while I was asleep.

It's funny how we tend to let go of the bad memories and hold on to the good ones. In spite of everything we had been through, we were still very blessed. We had a beautiful son together, and there were a lot of wonderful memorable years. Deep down inside, I longed for the old Jeff to come back.

Chapter 32

Hitting the Wall

The home inspection passed, with only a few minor things left to repair. At the buyer's request, the closing was moved up a few weeks to July 20, 2006.

I moved in with Joan a few weeks before closing. We decided that Butkis would stay with Jeff and Taz would stay with me. I had to find a home for Sasha (my Leopard Bengal Cat), which was very hard to do. I had her with me for almost nine years.

A few weeks before the closing, Jeff was coming back from the store and had an accident in the Mercedes. He was only one block from the house and it wasn't his fault. In fact, the guy who hit Jeff admitted fault. Jeff was shaken up and asked me to come to the scene of the accident. The Mercedes wasn't drivable and had to be towed, so I called AAA and our insurance company.

After getting the car towed to the body shop and explaining that Jeff was leaving right after the closing, they said they would have it ready by the time Jeff was ready to leave for California. In the meantime, he rented a new silver Dodge Charger.

I was back and forth between Joan's house, my storage unit and the apartment. I had to help pack the rest of the stuff. With Jeff injured again, there was nobody else to help me. We were about ten days away from closing. As I came down the stairs from the apartment on my way to the storage unit, I heard a loud bang.

I ran into the garage and found Jeff passed out in the driver's seat.

The car engine was still running. It looked like he had hit the garage wall trying to pull in and then was stopped (thank God) by the workbench in front. There was pink stuff coming out of his mouth. I called his name but there was no response at all. I looked down in between the two seats and saw that the car was still in the drive position, and the radio was blasting.

There was a large scrape and dent in the front left of the Charger where he had hit the wall. The driver's window down, I knew I had to get the car turned off, so I put my head and right arm through the window and tried to reach inside the car far enough to put the car in park. But my arm was too short and I couldn't reach it. Jeff's head was slumped down and in my way so I tried one more time to wake him up.

"Jeff, Jeff, wake up!"

He opened one eye and looked at me with a half-grin smile, then passed out again. There was a MacDonalds' bag and several prescription drug bags in the passenger seat. I realized that the pink stuff coming out of his mouth was a strawberry shake he got from McDonalds.

Jeff's doctors at the pain management clinic randomly checked Jeff's urine when he went to get his monthly check-up and scripts. His urine showed only one of his prescriptions in his system–that and the pot he smoked. Jeff and the doctor got into an argument because the doctor said he wasn't giving him anymore meds. Jeff got angry and said he hit something in the office on the way out.

He came home furious. I suggested that he call Dr. Mayo or his family doctor and let them know of his situation, because he was about to drive across the country. He couldn't drive by himself without medication. I also knew he had to be coherent at the closing to sign the papers on the house. I asked him several times over the next few days if he had been able to get any of the doctors to give him anything. He kept telling me no. Until today...

"Jeff, I need your help. I need you to wake up and put the car in park."

There was still no response. I couldn't leave him like this and I knew I had to turn the engine off. I decided to go for it and climb thru the drivers' window. First, I reached in to turn off the ignition, but it wouldn't turn off because the car was in the drive position. I was half in the car on my stomach and half out with my feet dangling in the air. I tried to put the gear knob in park again, but I was still in an awkward position. I forced myself in a little further and knew this was my only chance to shove it into park. It took everything I had. I shoved and squeezed the handle.

It wasn't enough. I had only managed to put the care in reverse, and now the car started backing out of the garage. I knew if I wasn't able to shift it into park, my legs and back would be crushed. I called out for God to help me, and desperately shoved and pushed with everything I had in me. As I finally hit the park position, the car lunged forward and I felt something pop. It was my rib cage.

I turned the key in the ignition off and slowly pushed myself up and slid out of the window. I was hurt. Jeff was snoring. With the engine off and the keys in my hand, I decided to let him stay in the car. It was apparent he had gotten his meds from someone. I looked at the RX bags and saw it was from Dr. Mayo. He would have to sleep it off in the car.

I called him the following day to see how he was. I told him what had happened and he told me he didn't remember the incident at all. He said he would check and see what kind of damage the car had sustained. I was worried about his blackouts. They were happening more frequently and we didn't understand why. Several months before, I had taken him to get a brain scan, but he never went back for the results.

He claimed he never got any medication from Dr. Mayo and he was going cold turkey. I wasn't sure if he really believed he didn't get anything or if he was lying to me to get me to feel sorry for him. Either way, I had to let it go.

Later (February 2009) we would learn that the Duragesic Patches that Jeff's doctors had prescribed for seven plus years had been recalled seven times. Over 120 deaths had occurred, due to a manufacturer's defect, which allowed an excessive amount of Fentanyl to get into the body, creating an overdose. It occurred to us that this could be responsible for Jeff's blackouts and shallow breathing. Also, the combination of the patches, Valium, Soma and Percodan could have killed him. The black box warning specifically stated NOT to combine these drugs when using Duragesic Patches. No doctor or pharmacist had warned us, either. They just kept writing and filling the prescriptions or could it be something that neither one of could have imagined.

The Mayflower moving van finally arrived on Wednesday, July 19, at eight in the morning. They were three days late, which meant that getting the house clean and ready for the final walk through was going to require me to be cleaning all night. The final walk-through was scheduled for nine the following morning, with the July 20 closing at eleven. Jeff thought the movers would only be there a few hours, but except for a few things that Travis and I were taking, they had the whole house to load.

I had been in and out all day, trying to do as much as I could, but it had rained and they tracked dirt in everywhere and made a complete mess. Jeff hadn't done any real deep cleaning after I stopped going down to the house. I had the two apartments, the workshop, the art room, and another little storage room all cleaned out of my stuff. Along with the main house, Jeff still had stuff to be cleaned out in all of those areas, including two of the garages.

Around five that afternoon, I heard the moving van finally pull out and I went downstairs to talk to Jeff.

I saw Travis. "Where's Dad?"

"Dad already left."

"What?"

"Dad left when the moving van left and is on his way to Cookie and Linda's."

"He didn't even say goodbye. Twenty-six years of being together and he didn't even say goodbye?" I looked at Travis in disbelief.

Travis and his friend, Hudson, looked at me–also in disbelief. I don't even think Jeff realized what he had done. Then it hit me; maybe it was too emotional for him. That would make more sense. If he didn't have to face it, he wouldn't have to deal with it. Still, it didn't make it hurt any less.

I started running around like a chicken with my head cut off. The house was filthy inside. Anything he didn't want to take, he just left there. I started to panic because I had no idea where was I going to put everything. The garbage can was already overflowing in the alley. Travis and Hudson took out what they could.

I called Jeff on his cell and left a message, but he didn't return my call. I sat down on the living room floor and looked around the room. I still had to vacuum, mop, clean all the toilets, the refrigerator—which was still half-full of stuff, not to mention all the stuff that was still in the garages. I did all I could. My back and neck were aching. At half past eleven that night I grabbed Taz and we went home. I was back at five in the morning taking stuff to the dumpster. At nine, one of the buyers showed up. She could see that I was very distraught.

She was very kind. "Brandi, Don't worry about the stuff in the garage for now. I'm not going to be back here for another week. I'll leave you a garage door opener and you can have an extra week to get your stuff out."

I was so relieved. "Thank you so much. The movers were three days late showing up and only arrived yesterday morning."

The buyers signed off on the walk-through. I rechecked to make sure everything was out of the main house and placed the key on the kitchen counter. Then everything hit me at once. It was really happening. The house Jeff wanted so desperately two years before was closing. Jeff was moving back home to California.

I looked at my watch. Taz would have to go with me to the closing. When Taz and I pulled in to the title company, Jeff was sitting in the Escalade. Jeff and Travis switched cars. The bigger vehicle would be easier on Butkis. Jeff got out like nothing had happened and we walked in together as husband and wife.

It wasn't as awkward as I thought it would be while we were outside, but when we went inside my emotions began to run wild. I still loved Jeff so much, but I couldn't watch him self-destruct anymore. I hoped that the trip to California would be a healing process for him and his family. The closing went well.

Jeff had decided to have one of his best friends from high school, Danny, fly out from California and drive back with him. There was relief for me in that. I didn't think Jeff was in any condition to drive across country by himself.

We had made plans to get together before he left, but he stiffed me at the last moment. Our friends had a going away party for him and invited Travis and Danny. He told me later how much that had meant to him. Then he was gone. Twenty-six years of being together was over.

Chapter 33

Never Give Up

A month before Jeff moved he asked me to put together a separation agreement, however he decided to wait and review it after he got back to California. We talked on the phone over the next few months and he indicated that he would sign it if I give up the NFL benefits I would be entitled to upon his death. Because of all of our medical bills, bankruptcy, and everything, Jeff's NFL pension was the only thing we had left, except for the small amount of proceeds we had split from the sale of our house.

I told him there was no way, because if something happened to him, I had no retirement, no other pension to fall back on. But I wanted to maintain a relationship with him because of our son. He said if I would sign off on the death benefits, he would get Travis and me an additional life insurance policy. I thought that was fair, so I agreed.

Jeff had the NFL send me the paperwork to sign. The paperwork clearly stated that if I signed off, there was no going back. Thinking I had an insurance policy coming, I signed off.   Jeff said later he never agreed to those terms. I was devastated but I had to let it go. My concentration moved to our son. Travis decided to go back to school in the fall and asked me to help pay for it. I told him I would help him pay for his rent, St. Pete College, and for his books. That's all I could afford. He changed jobs and worked security a few nights a week at an upscale place in Tampa and as a personal trainer at

Gold's Gym.

While he was at Gold's he met a guy named RC. RC was in training and preparing for the Tampa Bay Storm, a highly successful arena football team in Tampa that had four world championships.

To my surprise, after working with RC for seven or eight months, Travis really got into football and decided to try out for the Storm with RC. For Travis to say that, meant to me that he really thought he could play for the Storm.

I told him, "If you feel you're ready, go for it."

In November of 2006, His father was being inducted into his high school Hall of Fame in Turlock. The school was also celebrating their 100th year anniversary. I thought it would be nice to plan a trip for Travis to be there. He was excited and eager to tell his Dad about his plans to try out for the Storm.

Once he was in Turlock, Jeff told Travis, "There is no way you are ready for the pros in seven or eight months' time. Let me have some coaches look at you and see what you got."

The next day, Jeff had a few coaches look at Travis. They were very impressed with what they saw, and said to Jeff, "If you give us a year with him, he should be able to go wherever he wants."

Travis now had a lot of decisions to make. I thought it would be good for him to be with his Dad. Travis worshipped his father and like every young adult still wanted his father's acceptance and every pro-athlete father wants their son to follow in their footsteps

When I was doing the radio show, I had Travis and his roommate, Sam, talking about the transition from high school to college.

One of my questions during the show was, "Who was your hero and why?"

Travis immediately said that his father was his hero because of everything he had been through. I was very moved, but disappointed to later learn that Jeff had not listened to the show.

Six months after my job with the real estate agency started, it came to an abrupt end. Economics were forcing them to cut back on payroll and they decided to start having other agents volunteer their time and do the training. Forced to start living off my savings and alimony from Jeff, I decided to join another agency so I could practice real estate again and try to bring in some extra income. The real estate market took a major nose-dive and I took a part-time job with my girlfriend as her personal assistant. Everyone seemed to be going through tough times.

A few weeks into the Christmas holidays, Travis was still thinking about the move. While I was shopping for stocking stuffers, I came upon something called The Decision Maker. It was a round steel ball magnet and you could swing it like a pendulum and ask it questions. I bought one for Travis. We had an early Christmas because he was going to California to spend it with his Dad and grandparents. When he opened it up, he started smiling.

"Maybe this will help you make that decision on going to California or not. Either way son, I'm here. You know I love you. This is something you and only you can decide."

I sent gifts to Jeff, Jeff's parents and Travis's godparents. It was my first Christmas without Jeff or Travis and an emotional one. My girlfriend, Cay, and her boyfriend from Naples came up and spent Christmas Eve with me at the house. The next day, a few of my friends made Christmas dinner and I spent Christmas Day with them. For the first time, I knew what my mother went through when I was living in California and she was here by herself.

Whether or not my gift to Travis helped him make any decisions or not, I don't know, but right after Christmas, Travis decided he would make the move to California.

I don't know if Christmas had been an emotional one for Jeff, but December 31, 2006, I got a call from him. He was in a good mood and excited that Travis was moving out there.

Then he said, "Since Travis made the decision to move to California, I really wish you would think about making the move out here for the next two years. I found a house in Peacock Estates and if you were here and I wasn't paying you alimony, we could afford to buy it. I don't understand why you don't want to try and make our marriage work. I've changed, and I've gotten off all the patches and pain medication–and pot is legal here with a prescription."

"Jeff you know how much I love you. I wanted to try and see if we could work things out a few months back but you wouldn't agree on marriage counseling, drug rehab or medicine to treat your manic depression and mood swings."

I even agreed at one point to come and spend a few weeks with him at the house after his parents left for Arizona. He called and changed his mind, saying it would never work out. His up and down mood swings were still evident.

"Well, think about it, Brandi. There would be conditions that you would have to abide by. I wish we could just meet in a bar like we had never met before and start over."

I miss you, too, and I wish we could just meet in a bar and start over. I have to think about it."

"Okay," he said. "Just don't wait too long. I need to know if I can make an offer on this house."

I couldn't think about anything else that day. I prayed about it and asked God for guidance. It was as if the devil was on one shoulder and an angel was on the other. Part of me wanted to call him back and say yes, I want to move out and be with you and Travis, but the other part of me kept going back to the last twenty-six years of emotional chaos.

January 1, New Years Day, 2007, I had my answer. It was a day of new beginnings and I faxed him a letter. Maybe if he had told me how much he still loved me or missed me, it would have been a different letter–if he would agree to get on the proper anti-depressants. Instead, I felt he was more interested in the house; maybe it was his way of saying I still love you. As the last of the paper went through my fax machine, I questioned whether I had done the right thing. You don't love someone that many years and get over them in a day, but for now, I couldn't make the move.

We discussed several times over the next few months about whether or nor not to file for divorce or to just stay legally separated. During one of our conversations, he said, "Why don't we just hold off on filing. Neither one of us are in a hurry. You're not planning on getting married anytime soon are you?"

"No, are you?"

"No."

"Well, we should revise the separation agreement. If we ever decide to file, I have talked to an attorney here that Joe Zammataro recommended and we can just split the cost."

"Sounds good," Jeff said. "I don't know how to fill out all the paperwork anyway."

"Great, I'll revise the separation agreement and get it out right away."

Travis decided to wait until the end of March to make the move to California. Once he had committed to go, Jeff had the coaches ready to work with him as soon as he got there.

In April of 2007, I threw Travis a going away party with all of his friends at the house. I flew Errol Schmall, another friend of Travis's, out from Turlock to drive back with him.

As they pulled out of the driveway, it was hard to keep that rah-rah smile on my face. For a moment, I wanted to pack my things and say wait for me. Family is everything to me. But reality set in, and for now I prayed that God would surround them and get them there in one piece.

A week later, after Travis was getting settled in at his grandparent's house, I got a call from Dave Smith, Travis's basketball coach at Canterbury.

" Hi Brandi, How are you?"

Travis was being inducted into Canterbury's High School Hall of Fame. Travis couldn't be there, and I was honored when Travis asked me if I would accept the award on his behalf. He wrote a very moving acceptance speech and after reading it, there wasn't a dry eye in the house, including mine. I called Jeff a few weeks later to see how Travis was doing.

"I'm at my attorney's office filing the divorce papers and I'll have to call you back."

"I thought we had decided not to file right now."

"Well I decided to go ahead. My attorney said it will be easier for me to file here, so if you contested anything I wouldn't have to travel there."

With that comment, I was dumbfounded. Did he not remember

the conversation we had saying that we were not going to file, or was he planning to file all along and was just waiting for his six month legal residency to take place? I called my attorney in St. Petersburg and went in for a consult. He told me that if I wanted to contest it, I could, as this was the last place we last resided together. After thinking about it for a few hours, I decided to let it stand. In a later conversation, Jeff told me he had run into a gal he knew in high school and they had started dating.

On May 9, 2007, my birthday, I was served with my divorce papers. It was a very emotional day until my girlfriend's dog, where I was house-sitting, got up on the table and chewed the papers up.

A few weeks later, I happened to tune into Bryant Gumbel's show, interviewing Chris Nowinski about his book, "Head Games." Chris graduated from Harvard, where he played college football. He didn't make it to the NFL, but determined to stay in some line of sports, became a professional wrestler with the WWE, and was known as Chris "Harvard." After sustaining multiple concussions in both football and wrestling, his career came to an abrupt end.

After his last concussion, Chris began having problems with his memory, as well as constant headaches and occasional depression.

Only after being treated by a top neurosurgeon who specialized in concussions did Chris begin to understand his symptoms were side effects of multiple concussions he sustained over many years, and now has turned his personal struggles into a quest to educate others.

Bryant Gumbel's show also interviewed former NFL player, John Mackey, who suffers from front-temporal dementia. My heart poured out to John and his wife. John passed away August 2011.

Bryant's interview turned to another former NFL player, Ted Johnson, who hadn't shaved or bathed in eleven days. The only reason he was clean today, was because he had agreed to do this interview. He would make plans and stiff people, because emotionally he couldn't be around other people. His behavior also became more irrational over time.

As I listened, I grabbed a piece of paper and began to list the symptoms of multiple concussions: severe headaches, manic depression, bipolar, suicidal, violent tendencies, addiction to prescription drugs, becoming a recluse, not being able to function on a daily basis, profuse sweating, and possible dementia, Alzheimer's and Parkinson's disease later in life.

The Holy Spirit came all over me. Were the emotional problems that Jeff was experiencing, which contributed to the demise of our marriage, not what I thought they were, but after effects from playing in the NFL? I knew I had to learn more about concussions, so I googled Chris Nowinski on the Internet. I found one of his websites and emailed him.

I thought to myself, "God, if I am supposed to get involved in this, please give me a sign."

Within twenty-four hours, I got an email back from Chris. We made arrangements to have a phone conversation the following Monday afternoon. Monday morning, while I was watching the news on TV, I saw Mike Ditka and Joe Delemeirre talking about the upcoming NFL congressional hearings and how the NFL wasn't paying players for the disabilities they sustained from football.

I wanted to learn more about the hearings, so I contacted Ditka's organization, called the Gridiron Greats and left a message for their executive director, Jennifer Smith. After talking to Chris that afternoon at our scheduled appointment, he reconfirmed that I needed to contact Jennifer Smith and suggested that I come to the congressional hearings.

Chris was trying to get the effect of concussions recognized by the NFL and said he would see me in Washington. Jennifer Smith called me back a few days later and invited me to the press conference that the Gridiron Greats were having at the Washington Press Club before the hearings. She told me that Congresswoman Linda Sanchez was heading up the hearings.

I contacted Congresswoman Sanchez's office and asked if I could speak on behalf of the wives. One of her interns told me that the players who were giving their testimony had already been chosen, but said they welcomed any additional written testimony. I emailed my written testimony to her assistant.

I thought that maybe my testimony could inspire and give hope to someone else. The Gridiron Greats press conference at the Washington Press Club was very emotional. I met Mike Ditka, Mercury Morris, Joe Delemiere, Bernie Parrish, Brian and Autumn DeMarco, Brent and Gina Boyd, Mike Mosely, and Sandy Unitas in the VIP room prior to the conference.

Tears ran down my face as I held Autumn's hand, while we listened to her husband Brian, tell their story of how he had been fighting for his NFL disability pension for four years. In desperation, Autumn contacted the Gridiron Greats for help.

Brent Boyd and his wife Gina had only been married three years, but Gina already knew what it was like to live with a disabled former NFL player who had sustained multiple concussions.

Mike Mosely, who played with Jeff at Buffalo, wouldn't come to the hearings and only spoke at the press conference, because he was too emotional and couldn't handle being around people. Mike had won his disability income, only to have it taken away later. I knew firsthand what that was about. Jeff won his arbitration, only to have it taken away. He couldn't handle being around people he didn't know.

After the hearings, Joe DeLemierre, who also played with Jeff at Buffalo, told me in the car on the way back to the hotel that if it wasn't for his wife, he wouldn't know what he would have done in the early years after he left football.

Autumn and Brian, and their two small children, were living in a storage shed and hadn't eaten anything except crackers for three days, when Jennifer Smith knocked on their door. She got the children food, helped them get into an apartment and Brian into drug rehab. Brian had a $1,000 a month prescription drug habit. He had both of his elbows crushed and seventeen bones in his back broken while playing in the NFL for the Jacksonville Jaguars.

The most heartbreaking story, one that really touched home for me, was Garrett Webster's. He is the son of Hall of Famer, Mike Webster. At the press conference, he spoke these words:

"My father died alone on a cold floor, next to the toilet, from a heart attack. There was no wife, no children around. My father was so confused one time, he went into the kitchen and peed in the oven. I think the only reason he didn't kill himself was because he was too demented to figure out how to pull a trigger."

Everyone's emotions were running deep. I thought of all of the times when Jeff was incapacitated and did crazy things–many of which I barely touch on in this book.

Mercury Morris, Brent Boyd, Johnny Unitas's wife, Sandy, and a few other players got up and told their story. Each one was more moving than the last.

After the press conference, I got a chance to speak with Chris Nowinski. It was so nice to meet him in person. Here was this tall, good-looking, twenty-eight year old man who appeared to be so healthy–but who has already lived a lifetime of injury to his body. So have all of these players.

When former NFL player, Andre Waters, committed suicide in November of 2006, he was only forty-four years old. An autopsy, which Chris was responsible for arranging, with permission from Andre's sister, found he had the brain of an eighty-five year old man.

I found that Bernie Parrish and two other players had filed a class action lawsuit on behalf of all of the retired NFL players. By the end of the press conference, I knew I was supposed to be there.

As we were leaving and heading over to the hearings, I asked Jennifer if I could help carry anything to the car. Outside, I watched Brian slowly and painfully get into the passenger side of the car. As I sat in the back seat with Autumn, I couldn't take my eyes off of the back of Brian's head. All I could see was Jeff. Years of emotions were welling up and unraveling again. Then we were at the hearings.

Inside the congressional hearing, it was standing room only. There were many players who showed up who were not at the press conference. At one, the hearings began. As I listened to each story, my heart ached. Every story I listened to reinforced my reason for being there–especially after meeting the other wives. Wives from the NFL Wives Club who, like me, were the unknown soldiers and back-bone of the family unit.

We protect our husband's pride. We protect our shame of having to live false lives, hiding the truth from the communities we live in.

From all the beautiful letters Jeff wrote to me over the years, I know that he was upset at what I was literally thrown into the day he left football, and after the gunshot accident.

I finally understood, and believe that Jeff had no control over a lot of his actions. I believe that his emotional problems were a result of the eleven-plus concussions he sustained while playing college and professional football. Every story that I listened to wasn't just my story, but the same story, told over and over again.

Jeff and his fellow NFL comrades have paid an enormous price for such short-lived glory. They would all be back on the field in an instant, because they love the game. They are all wonderful men who were unfortunately lost on the battlefield of the NFL.

The devastating and long-term effects of concussions have to be recognized by the NFL and other institutions. The evidence is mounting that seemingly minor concussions have immediate and permanent negative consequences, and may set the neurodegenerative processes in motion much sooner than is now believed.

As a group, NFL players have a far greater risk of developing Alzheimer's disease than do other males of the same age in the United States. Retired players with three or more concussions are five times more likely to be diagnosed with mild cognitive impairment (MCI) than are retired players who never reported having had a concussion.

Former NFL player Harry Carson stated in Chris Nowinski's book, that he started to notice changes as a commentator. He would lose his train of thought. He was sensitive to bright lights and noise, and suffered bouts of depression. Carson was diagnosed with post-concussion syndrome two years after retiring.

In 2002, Hall of Famer Mike Webster died at the age fifty. His autopsy revealed that he suffered from a degenerative neurological disease caused by repeated head trauma. Webster's doctors said that his concussions damaged his frontal lobe, causing cognitive dysfunction.

It was also confirmed that he had structural damage to his brain, consistent with chronic traumatic encephalopathy (CTE), or punch-drunk syndrome, often found in boxers. Five of five NFL players over the age of twenty-five have been diagnosed with CTE. It was the first time CTE had ever been found in a professional football player.

At times Mike took a laundry list of drugs: Prozac for depression, Paxil for anxiety, Ritalin or Dexedrine to keep him calm, Klonopin to prevent seizures and Elddepryl, a drug indicated for patients who suffer severe Parkinson's disease. By 1997, he told a doctor that his daily headaches were "blowing his head off." He would ask his children to use a black Taser gun to stun him into unconsciousness so he could sleep. His former teammate, Terry Long, died at age forty-five. Terry's autopsy revealed he suffered from the same neurodegenerative ailment.

The Center for the Study of Retired Athletes (CSRA) found that the rate of depression among ex-NFL players reporting three or more concussions was more than triple the rate of those without concussions. Seventy-six percent of the former NFL players, based on that study, said that depression "often" or "sometimes" limits their activities of daily living. And the former players' frequency of "feeling sad, nervous, mixed emotions or under stress," correlated strongly with their concussion histories.

The families suffer and, like me, don't understand the irrational behavior. The brain, unlike some other parts of our body, cannot regenerate.

Disability benefits have to be awarded. We fought sixteen years to get Jeff's disability benefits, and he was still never recognized as being fully disabled from professional football–something I don't think he will ever get over. The NFL has to do what they promised Jeff and these other players a long time ago, and that is to "take care of their own."

I will always love Jeff. We have a son together and that tie will never be broken. I know that God took me on this journey so that I could be a testimony to help others come to a better understand of the after effects of concussions, to help other families and the need to stand up and fight the NFL for better pensions and continued medical after they leave the game.

I pray that he finds the peace and joy he longs for. He is a wonderful man and someone who will always be in my heart. Who knows, maybe Jeff and I will meet at another bar and start over. Only God knows for sure.

Hopefully I have shown you that no matter what your story is, you must keep the faith and know that with God on your side anything is possible. Surely if God takes you to it, God will get you through it. Fight for what you believe and Never Give Up.

Resources

I want to thank Chris Nowinski for the research that he did to help him understand his own bout with concussions and all the work he continues to do to educate coaches and parents.

If you or a loved one has suffered from concussions, severe headaches, depression, prescription drug addiction or if you have thought about suicide, please learn more and use these resources:

For more information on:

Manic Depression (also known as Bipolar):
>   www.bipolar.com
>   www.knowmydepression.com
>   www.allaboutlifechallenges.org
>   www.everydayhealth.com

For support groups go to:
>   www.ndmda.org
>   www.bipolar.com

For more information on concussions:
>   www.sportslegacy.org
>   www.mayoclinic.com/health/concussion

For a free copy of TBI Coaches Toolkit:
>   www.cdc.gov/ncipc/tbi/coaches_tool_kit.htm
>   Head Games by Christopher Nowinski

NFL Disability References:
>   www.dignityafterfootball.org
>   www.gridirongreats.org
>   www.retiredplayers.org
>   www.davepear.com
>   www.playersforjustice.org
>   www.footballsummit.com (new 2009)

Author Bio

Brandi Winans is an Author, Inspirational Speaker/Facilitator/ former radio and television host. Growing up in St. Pete Beach,Fla., her love as a child was snorkeling, collecting shells and fossils with her father.

She learned first hand the values of integrity and character from the former Marine. In her teen years, her love of horses, acting and dancing drew her to Southern California where she finished college majoring in Communications and Psychology.

Her passion is helping others especially teens and young adults discover their natural born gifts and talents through her unique Life skills Seminars.

She continues her work as an NFL Advocate for pre-93 former NFL players. Her "I believe in you attitude" makes her a sought after speaker. Her family is her greatest blessing.

Visit her at: www.brandiwinans.com

Credits

The Wannabe Seminars© 2002, 2008, 2011
The Stepping Stones of Life/Audio CD/Workbook© 2005
Harness the Power of your Passion © 2011
Co-Author: Harness the Power© 2011((with NSA-CF Academy)
Former radio Host- WTBN Christian Talk Radio.
Former actor/model
Education/Specialized Training/Certifications:
Santa Moncia College-emphasis on Communication/ Psychology
National Speakers Association Academy Graduate
Department of Juvenile Justice Volunteer Chaplains Program 2009
Success for Teens Facilitator, 2010—present
D.i.S.C. Behavioral Assessments Facilitator
St. Pete Chamber of Commerce Entrepreneurial Academy 2006
Leadership Mastery Course- How to Challenge Yourself and Others
      to Greatness—Dale Carnegie
Sylva Business Programs–Stress Management/Internal Motivation/
      Self Improvement
Graduate Source One Mortgage College
Licensed Realtor- National Asset Mangers 1990-present
      (Sweat Hog Graduate, RE Trainer/Facilitator)
Member:
Board of Director Day For Our Children (Founder) 1992—present
Board of Director and Past Guild President Boys and Girls of The
      Suncoast 2004—present
Department of Juvenile Justice Steering Committee
      (Circuit 6) 2007—present
Advisory Board for Charles Britt Halfway House 2009—present
National Speakers Association Central Florida,
Pinellas County Schools Speakers Bureau
Florida Writers Association

Jeff Winans
Offensive Guard
Tampa Bay Bucs 1978

Jeff and Gene Upshaw
Oakland Raiders 1980

Shari, Sandra and Jeff Winans
1954

Jeff, Modesto Junior
College 1969

Jeff's Birthday, Buffalo, NY
1975

Nina Bynum (Jeff's Aunt),
Jeff and Sandra Winans
1976

Jeff and John Matuzak
Roommates
Oakland Raiders 1980

Sandra, Brandi, Travis and Jeff
Turlock, California
1986

Jeff and Travis
St. Petersburg Florida
1990

Travis and College Football Coach
Modesto Junior College ~ 2009

Brandi and Sandra Winans
2004

Melting in his arms with
love as deep as the sea

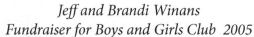

Jeff and Brandi Winans
Fundraiser for Boys and Girls Club 2005

Made in the USA
Las Vegas, NV
25 February 2021